GO

Beginning a Kids' Outreach Ministry

Rachael Groll

Warner Press, Inc
Warner Press and Warner Press logo are trademarks of Warner Press, Inc

Go: Beginning a Kids' Outreach Ministry
Written by Rachael Groll

Copyright ©2017 Rachael Groll

Cover and layout copyright ©2017 Warner Press Inc

Scripture quotations used in this book were taken from the following:

- (ESV) *ESV® Bible* (*The Holy Bible, English Standard Version®*), copyright © 2001 by Crossway Bibles, a publishing ministry of Good News Publishers. Used by permission. All rights reserved.
- (KJV) *Holy Bible, King James Version*. Public Domain.
- (MSG) THE MESSAGE, copyright © 1993, 1994, 1995, 1996, 2000, 2001, 2002 by Eugene H. Peterson. Used by permission of NavPress. All rights reserved. Represented by Tyndale House Publishers, Inc.
- (NASB) *New American Standard Bible®* (NASB), Copyright © 1960, 1962, 1963, 1968, 1971, 1972, 1973, 1975, 1977, 1995 by The Lockman Foundation. Used by permission. www.Lockman.org
- (NIV) HOLY BIBLE, NEW INTERNATIONAL VERSION®. NIV®. Copyright © 1973, 1978, 1984, 2011 by Biblica, Inc.®. Used by permission. All rights reserved worldwide.
- (NKJV) *New King James Version®*. Copyright © 1982 by Thomas Nelson. Used by permission. All rights reserved.
- (NLT) *Holy Bible, New Living Translation* copyright© 1996, 2004, 2007 by Tyndale House Foundation. Used by permission of Tyndale House Publishers Inc., Carol Stream, Illinois 60188. All rights reserved.
- (NLV) *New Life Version*, copyright © 1969 Christian Literature International.

All rights reserved. No part of this publication may be reproduced, stored in a retrieval system, or transmitted in any form or by any means—electronic, mechanical, photocopy, recording, or any other—except for brief quotations in printed reviews, without the prior permission of the publisher.

Requests for information should be sent to:
Warner Press, Inc
2902 Enterprise Drive
Anderson, IN 46013
www.warnerpress.org

Editors: Robin Fogle and Karen Rhodes
Cover: Curtis Corzine
Layout Design: Katie Miller

ISBN: 978-1-59317-943-4
This book is also available in e-book format.

Printed in USA

Table of Contents

1. All In 7
2. Qualified. 17
3. What the What? 27
4. Love Kids—Love Their Families 39
5. Lessons in Grace 53
6. Success or Significance. 63
7. Words. 73
8. Fear or Fight. 81
9. Hungry. 91
10. Obedience and Expectation 101
11. Remarkable. 111
12. Resilience 119

Appendix A: Sidewalk Sunday School Lessons 129
Appendix B: Sidewalk Sunday School Games 157
Appendix C: Leadership Training Outlines 167

To Aiden.

At the moment we met, I knew God had something special in store for you. You are a constant prayer in my heart. It's because of you that the Kingdom has been changed.

1. ALL IN

"You need a truck. We need to get you a truck."

I had no idea what he was talking about. I was sitting in my pastor's office, describing to him some of the children I had met the previous night. I had seen at least 50, but there were many more attached to those 50, if you considered siblings and friends.

"You mean a bus," I responded, thinking he just hadn't had enough coffee yet.

"No. I mean a bread truck," he said, as he immediately sat down and started to Google truck images.

Still confused, I watched as he pulled up pictures of a bread truck and described how we could cut the side out of it and make it into a stage that pulls down. Once we had a truck, we could "DO" church outside on the sidewalk.

Immediately, the wheels in my brain started turning....

• • •

I almost hadn't gone. I was preparing for an event, a Fall Harvest Party, and I had some leftover flyers from Sunday morning. The event was Thursday, so I was just going to throw them out. Our church secretary, Louise, suggested I take them down to a particular neighborhood in our community. To be honest, my first thought was, "NO WAY." That place was scary. There were drugs there. And lots of crime. And police. "And children," the Lord added. Ouch. I couldn't argue with that.

GO

"I'll go with you," Louise said. I thought maybe she could just take them for me. I had my young daughter with me. Surely I shouldn't be doing this.

"GO." The Lord very clearly, and very loudly, spoke into my heart. "Just go."

Taking a deep breath, I made plans with Louise to meet after work to take the flyers down into the low-income housing project. Truth be told, I avoided the place. I literally drove right past the entrance to it every single day. It was on the outskirts of town, as most of the housing projects were, so you didn't have to look at them if you didn't want to. And I didn't want to. My limited exposure to that area left me with a mixture of fear and disdain. I'm ashamed to say that I avoided the area because it reminded me too much of things I had tried so hard to forget—things I had buried deep down inside that I was unwilling to expose. Of course, God knew this, yet He still told me to go. So, out of obedience, I went. I put my emotions aside, and I walked, one step at a time, into what I would later realize was my greatest calling in life.

A couple months prior, I had traveled to Kenya on a mission trip and spent time with some incredible kids. The trip was life changing, and it opened my eyes to the need in our world. I came home with a renewed passion for the gospel and a burning desire to return to Africa. As I walked along the sidewalk in the housing project and was surrounded by children, I quickly realized I had missed the fact that we had a mission field literally a couple of miles from my house. Why hadn't I recognized this before? How could I have missed these kids? Why didn't they ever come to church? Why weren't there churches or ministries reaching out to them? SO many questions flooded my mind, and I quickly became conscious that God was up to something. They, like any other kids, were desperate for love and attention, and the Jesus in me was telling me that He had work for me to do here.

One little boy, Ty, was about two years old, and he followed me everywhere I went. Where were his parents? Where did he live? Why wasn't anyone looking for him? As I looked around, I quickly realized that many of these kids were largely unsupervised and desperate for love and attention. I was giving out small flyers, inviting them to an event we were having at the church. The flyer was colorful and bright, and many of the kids were simply excited to be given something free that they could keep. A piece of paper. I had nothing else to give them.

Little did I realize at that moment that I DID have something else to give them. God was opening my eyes and revealing that He had a plan and a purpose for this neighborhood—that these kids belonged to Him, and He was going to use me to reach them. I didn't know how. I didn't know why. All I knew was that He was working and moving and that I needed to figure out how to be a part of it.

Ty, jumping up and down very excitedly, said to me, "You never came here before! No one ever comes here! Can you stay? Can you come back?" His words pierced my heart. *"No one ever comes here."* I knew I had to come back. I would find a way to reach this area.

Many of the kids were excited to be invited to the party but had no transportation. The next day, I poured out my heart to our senior pastor, Ray. "We can start with a bus. Get a bus down there for Sunday morning. We can rent one, but we have to do more than that. We need to send something down there to where they live."

As my pastor started to describe his plan to get a truck, I started to realize he had the same things laid on his heart that I had on mine. So we committed to praying for these kids and started to figure out a way to reach them.

The first Sunday we sent a bus down, we got one lone rider, and it wasn't even a kid. She was a crazy cat lady who had been praying for a ride to church, and she was so excited that we came to get her.

GO

I was heartbroken. Not about the cat lady, I was glad she was coming to church. She definitely needed Jesus. But where were all the kids? I had gone down to the neighborhood during the week and invited tons of them. I honestly expected that we would need two buses. I thought we were going to fill up the first bus so quickly that we would need to send a Greyhound the second week. Not so much. I was so disappointed that I went to the bathroom and cried. As I sat there, doubting if I was even on the right track, I heard the Lord whisper to my heart, "Keep going." In that moment, I realized God had a plan bigger than that empty bus.

What's Your Empty Bus?

Maybe you have tried an outreach event before, and it wasn't well attended. Maybe you did some door-to-door evangelism only to find more doors slammed in your face than opened. Maybe you shared your heart, only to have it pierced. My physical eyes could not yet see it, but God had a plan and a purpose for the kids in that neighborhood, and it was going to take some resolve.

So many times, I think we look at a situation, and we start something—we step into a new calling—and we expect immediate results. Why? Because we live in a fast food, instant message culture that places the expectation of immediate gratification on the same shelf as hard won results. Perseverance and determination are no longer the standard formula for results in much of our society. Instead, we are trained to look for "likes" and "followers" and to consider our measure of success in terms of how quickly we can get others to respond. The empty bus was a moment God used to teach me that this ministry was going to take time. It would take time to break down walls that had been built, and I was going to have to do it one brick at a time.

The following week, I visited the kids again. I found my little buddy, Ty, and took him a Tootsie Roll. I watched some girls as they showed me how they could jump rope. I helped a little boy when he lost his grip on the monkey bars. I applauded a pop a wheelie, and I tied some shoes. That's all. The next Sunday we had 25 kids. I quickly realized my half hour in the neighborhood was the most valuable thing I had done all week. Connecting to kids in the form of meeting real needs was going to open the door for me to help them with their spiritual need. Being where they are. Staying close to the need so it could touch me, both physically and emotionally. Instead of insulating myself inside the four walls of the church, I was going to have to get out into the trenches and meet the needs where they were.

Throughout the winter, we ran a bus—sometimes two—down to the neighborhood on Sundays. We typically were getting anywhere from 15-40 kids. I was even prepared to send a third bus down because I knew close to 100 kids actually lived there. They just weren't coming on Sundays. Soon, the need became clear. We needed to take the church to them.

I had been waiting on a truck, but the reality was we were having a hard time finding one. Even if we found one for a good price, it would take a lot of work and time before we could get it fitted for a stage. So, after praying about how to start, we decided to just go. We picked a day and time, we got some helpers, and we started to plan what we were going to do. I had a really nice soundboard and speakers that were not being used at the church, which was a big blessing because I wouldn't have to spend any money for this necessary equipment. I made a playlist of songs kids loved. I made a candy wall of bubble gum, Airheads, and lollipops. I made some posters to keep track of points for some games we would play. I was ready. Armed with a popup tent, hula hoops, and some bubbles, we headed into the neighborhood. I didn't know what to expect, but I felt prepared with a fun program I thought the kids would like. We didn't even know if any kids would come. We didn't know if we were going to get kicked out. We also

GO

didn't know what we were doing or how it was going to work. But we did know Jesus, and we knew the kids needed to know Him too.

As we pulled into the neighborhood, we were met by a dozen or so kids, who were excitedly anticipating our arrival. They helped me unload my minivan and set up tarps on the ground. They rode their bikes around the block, yelling for their friends to "come to church." By the time we were set up and ready to go, we had at least 30 kids. I knew there were many more in the area, but this was a great start. My plan was to start amping up the speakers with some fun music to draw a crowd. Kids were excited. Our team was excited. We were doing it.... We were doing Sunday school on the sidewalk!

And then it happened. It started to rain. I'm not talking about a light summer shower. I'm talking monsoon. We don't ordinarily have monsoons in Meadville, Pennsylvania. The weather had not been calling for rain, but at the exact moment we were starting our program, the skies opened up and released a flood. The guys on our team quickly packed up all the electronic equipment. As I gathered the kids under the tent, I realized the rain had ruined my lesson and all my props. We couldn't play the games. The candy wall was soaked and thrown back into the van. The balloons were deflated on the ground. Everything I had planned for the day was suddenly out the window. I had none of the things I usually use on a Sunday morning.

Yet, I had everything I needed. I started to talk about how God's love was like that rain. He wanted them to be soaked in it, just like their clothes were. Every single child who was there that day in the rain under a leaky tent, clothes soaked through, gave their heart to Jesus. I had the privilege of praying with them as they laid down their rejection and insecurities and traded them for the hope of the gospel. We didn't need everything we thought we did. The reality was, all we needed was Jesus. He saw. He knew. And He moved. We sent the kids home for their own safety, and we packed up with promises to return the following week. I was overwhelmed with what had happened. I had planned and prayed. I gathered a team. I memorized songs. I made playlists. In the end, we used none of it. A verse came to mind:

> *For our struggle is not against flesh and blood, but against the rulers, against the authorities, against the powers of this dark world and against the spiritual forces of evil in the heavenly realms.*
> Ephesians 6:12 (NIV)

The enemy had done a good job of convincing people that neighborhood was hopeless. And in a sense, it was. It had no hope. That's why it needed Jesus. What happened that first day, very clearly, was a battle for the hearts of those kids.

I wish I could say the following week was better. The weather was better, for sure. We actually got to use our speakers and sound system. We played some fun games and had about 45 kids. However, as we were at the point of leading kids in prayer, right as we were teaching about salvation, we heard the brakes of a car coming to a screeching halt, a scream, and then silence. Within a few seconds, a little boy on a bike rode down to where we were and told us a child from across the street was coming to Sidewalk and was hit by a car. The driver wasn't paying attention, the child wasn't paying attention, and the parents were nowhere in sight.

As this child was splayed across the cement and we waited for an ambulance to arrive, I started to tear up. "What is going on, Lord?" I cried. I was heartbroken for this child.

As I looked at these small faces staring at me, I heard Him whisper again, "Keep going."

Taking a deep breath, I led the children in two prayers: one for our little friend who was badly injured and another for the kids who wanted to give their hearts to the Lord. They very easily saw that life was fragile. We didn't know what was going to happen that day or if

GO

our friend would live or die, but that terrible moment the enemy had purposed for tragedy became a moment God used to deliver hope. We had 15 more kids lay their lives in the hands of Jesus.

The truth was, things like car accidents happened in that neighborhood all the time. The kids weren't as shaken up as I was because they were desensitized to the reality of their harsh world. The enemy had a firm grip on this area, and we were tempted to just run away. But I have to believe that Christ's plan for redemption extends far beyond the four safe walls of a church. I have to believe that as followers of Christ we are called to take the light INTO the darkness, not to run away from it. We continued to go back at the same time every week and started to build real relationships with the families there. We visited on other days during the week and watched as the kids were not just coming one day a week to "church" as they called it, but were asking for Bibles and praying for their families.

About a month into our ministry, I felt led to teach a lesson on the Holy Spirit. We were starting with foundational concepts because many of the kids had never been to church and knew very little. We started with God and creation, then the Bible, then Jesus. So naturally, the Holy Spirit was next. I decided to teach them that the Holy Spirit was like an invisible super hero. They couldn't see Him, but He was there to help them. I did a simple activity to help them make it personal. I had them say hello to the Holy Spirit, and then had them say out loud, "Holy Spirit, You are welcome here." As they did, there was a noticeable change in the spiritual climate in that neighborhood. You could literally feel that God was moving in the hearts of those there.

From that day on, something had broken. I'm not even sure how to put it into words, but the resistance we had in the beginning was transformed into open hearts and doors. We still had challenges—don't get me wrong. An entire chapter of this book will describe some

GO

huge obstacles we had to overcome. But in the spiritual sense, we could see freedom—families being healed, addictions being broken, hearts being mended. Transformation. And it was just the beginning. God had, and has, a plan and a purpose in that neighborhood. And do you know what? He does in your community too. There is an area in your community that God is ready to move in; He just needs you to go with Him.

The Need Is the Call

If I am honest, I have to admit that when God called me to walk into the midst of unfamiliar territory, I didn't go because I felt called. I went because I was surrendered and obedient to the one who loved me the most. I would not have chosen that neighborhood had I been given the choice. But...GOD. God knew what He was doing when He placed me in that area. He knew the need I saw there would trigger something in me. It would remind me what it felt like to be abandoned. Rejected. Lonely. Scared. And those feelings would move me to a heart of compassion for kids going through the same thing. Someone who hadn't lived in that world, pitched a tent in the camp of rejection, and experienced those feelings might not understand how Jesus is the ONLY solution. See, I knew this about Him. He literally picked me up, turned me around, and set my feet on solid ground. He was my Savior, and I knew He could rescue them too. I saw the need, and I quickly realized the need IS the call. We can complicate that, but the reality is, there are kids in your town, your community, your neighborhood, who need Jesus. They don't need just a weeklong summer VBS program or a bus that comes through once a week to pick them up if they get up on time. They NEED Jesus. They need a personal encounter with the one who created them, who can speak into the dark parts of their hearts and exchange darkness for light. They need Him, and they need YOU to introduce them to Him. I know this

15

GO

type of outreach is hard. I know all about logistics and budgets, time constraints and red tape. *I know.* But I also know we have a God who pursues us, despite all the things that we put in His way. He pursues us in a way that overwhelms us when we realize how incredibly much we are loved. And how can we keep that good news away from those who are desperate for Him?

My hope is that you will take this book and use it as a guide to get moving in your own community. Throughout the book, I will be posing some questions for you to think about and reflect on. It might be beneficial to discuss these questions with your team. Then act on them. Even if you don't know what to do, still act. A lot of the groundwork in this type of ministry happens through trial and error. You keep what works, and you throw out what doesn't. We are now running multiple sites in our community. Each site is different, and we handle each site as a unique opportunity to minister to the needs of those who live there. There is no difference between my community and yours. Start praying about where to go, and be expectant that God WILL show you an area to start in. And then, just go.

Something to Think About:

Where do you see need in your community? Identify three key places that demonstrate need. These can be apartment complexes, housing developments, trailer parks, low-income neighborhoods, playgrounds, etc. Pray for God to reveal to you an area to begin praying for. If you are unaware of needy areas in your community, several resources are available that provide this information. You can start by calling your local county assistance office or other local community agencies listed in the phone book. Once you identify an area, start praying for the families that live there. As you commit to pray, God will give you a unique desire to start loving and ministering in that community. Prayer is what will maintain and sustain.

2. QUALIFIED

My father doesn't love me. At least, that's how it feels.

At a very young age, I learned the harsh lesson that my father had no interest in pursuing a relationship with me. Whether it was his addiction to alcohol or his own troubled childhood, some sort of barrier was always holding him back from even saying he loved me. He didn't spend any time with me, he didn't look me in the eyes—he barely spoke to me. No matter how well I did in school, no matter how great a job I had, no matter how impossible a fight I had won, a sad realization took the breath out of every victorious or proud word I would dare to speak—nothing would ever be good enough for my father.

In all fairness, my mom is the same way. Her addiction has always made it hard for me to have a healthy relationship with her. Both parents are absent from my life. After years of rejection from them, I finally stepped away after it started affecting my children. There was a time in my life when I constantly sought out the love that I truly don't think they are capable of giving. The unconditional love I have for my children is something I had always hoped for with my own parents. That desire kept me going back into the impossible, frustrating, abusive mess, in search of something that would make me whole. But somehow, being around them always took something more away from me.

GO

One day, my youngest daughter overheard a voicemail saying they were coming to see us. It was the first time we had heard from my parents in over eight months. The last time had been just before Christmas, when they promised to come over for dinner. We had presents wrapped, cookies baked, and expectations of a happy family Christmas. When the day was over and they hadn't come, when they hadn't called or even answered our calls, I knew what I was hoping for was something they probably weren't capable of. Even though there was disappointment, there were also presents and friends and Christmas movies, snowmen and lazy vacation days. My kids didn't know much different; my parents had never really been involved in their lives.

This time, however, was different. My youngest, who is always looking for the best in people, was standing in the kitchen, listening as I played the blinking message on the answering machine. I normally would keep her from that, so her heart wouldn't be broken when they didn't come. I knew not to expect them to keep promises and so did my older kids, but my youngest is impossibly hopeful. She has seen so many miracles that she lives in a state of expectancy—full of faith. She was a baby when I joined the staff at the church full time, so she has literally been raised there, surrounded by people who speak life over her and love her tremendously. So for her, this phone call was the answer to her little prayers for my parents to get their lives together.

As she counted down the days until they were supposed to come, I tried to warn her. She wouldn't hear of it, instead making them pictures and crafts to help show how much she wanted them in her life. My other children just kind of held their breath, knowing their grandparents probably wouldn't show up. When the day they were supposed to come arrived, I tried to busy her with books and crafts, but she waited anxiously by the door. As the time came and went, I tried to engage her in some of her favorite activities, and she refused. She just waited, looking out the window.

As I watched her heart go from hopeful excitement to bitter disappointment, I recognized what she felt. I sat down on the stairs behind her and curled her into a hug. As she started to cry, I did too. "I thought they loved me. I thought they would come," she said. Her little heart was broken. She didn't know rejection the way I did. For me, rejection was almost like an old friend who constantly knocked on the door to my heart while I tried to pretend I didn't hear. But for her—my beautiful, perfect, sweet, tender baby girl—this pain was something she had been protected from. As I held her through her tears, I realized this feeling of being unloved and unwanted causes suffering for so many people. I had been carrying it around my whole life. I didn't know quite what to do about it, but something rose up in me that day. A fierce love produces a fire inside a mama that is ignited when someone hurts her child. As I struggled through these emotions, thoughts, and feelings, I started to pray for God to give me some wisdom in how to navigate this new level of rejection. For me, the pain of watching my child's rejection was worse than the pain when it happened to me.

For a few weeks, the situation was at the tip of my tongue, the edge of my heart, and the front of my mind. While I was still in this emotional place, I had to attend a staff retreat. Our pastoral staff had taken a weekend to get away for a time of refreshing with our spouses. Towards the end of the weekend, with my heart still tender, we entered a time of worship and prayer together. As we did, I prayed for the kids in our ministry, for the adults on our teams, and for the impact on our community. I did not, however, dare to even think about those hurting parts of my heart that I had buried and pretended weren't there for the weekend.

GO

But you see, somehow, God knows when to extract those hurting pieces of our lives so that He can replace them with something better. As I was praying, God showed me something I had never seen before. This new season of leadership I was in had brought me quite a bit of growth in my walk with the Lord. I was starting to hear the Lord's voice much more clearly. But this moment? This moment was different. As I was in that room worshiping, surrounded by our team that loves Jesus, the Lord met me in my hurting place. In my spirit, I saw Him. He brought His face close to mine and touched my cheek. His eyes, the color of unconditional love and compassion and pain, met mine. "I," He said, almost in a whisper, "I will NEVER leave you!"

If you have never experienced the type of communication with Jesus that I'm talking about, then I don't really know how to explain it. It's not an audible voice you hear, it's not a rushing wind, it's not a burst of flames. It's a still, confident word that is pressed into the very place in your heart that needs it the most.

As I felt the words hit me, my tears released in my body what was happening in my spirit. There was something so profound about those couple of minutes. Years of pain, tears, and longing were suddenly filled with something that I didn't even know was missing. The love of my Creator, my Savior, Jesus had finally permeated every dark part of my heart. I think we all have some spots in our hearts like that—protected but wounded. It hurts too much to let anyone in there, so we put up walls and then pretend there isn't anything painful behind the wall. But you see, the one who made my heart was the very one who could heal it. The only one. No amount of love from my biological father would ever measure up to the love that would truly satisfy that craving for Jesus. It never could. I know that now.

• • •

You may be wondering why I chose to include such a personal story. I include it because I think you can relate. I include it because this is such an important concept to grasp. I include it because if you don't know it, you can't live it. **The only one who can ever truly satisfy your heart is the one who made it.** In Him, there is no depletion, only completion. Many of the kids we minister to come from homes that are taking more from them than they are giving. Kids need to *know* Jesus, not just know *about* Jesus. There's a difference. The difference is teaching a lesson or living the lesson. The difference is conflicting their minds or capturing their hearts. You see, when you talk about the Father who loves them, many of them don't even know what the love of a father is. But if you SHOW them the love of the Father, they will experience it in a way they will never forget. That's why so much of this ministry is based on relationship. The ministry that happens when you are tying shoes or changing bike tire chains or wiping away tears—that is what will open their little hearts. As you walk out faith in your own life, it will naturally overflow into theirs.

When I first started in this ministry, I felt like I was somehow an imposter. Here I was teaching the kids, watching transformation of lives and families, seeing hundreds of people come to faith in Christ, and I was secretly waiting for someone to jump out of the bushes and tell me that I did not have the resumé to be doing such a job. I felt like surely there was someone more qualified, with a better education, more public speaking experience, and a brilliant mind who was really supposed to be doing all of this. And yet, here I was, the one standing with the microphone. It took about a year or two before I realized perhaps God hadn't made a mistake and I was exactly where I belonged. There are still many days when I am not confident, that I silently pray for wisdom and words and boldness, even while standing in front of the kids. But I have realized some things along the way that I hope will encourage you as you seek God's wisdom in reaching out to the lost and hurting kids in your community....

GO

1. God Has Given You a REAL Message.

Nothing is wasted in the kingdom of God. Although I was just a mom when I first started out, I was also just a kid who had been neglected and abandoned. I knew from personal experience what it felt like to be cast aside. I knew the pain of crying myself to sleep and the impossible feeling of never being able to measure up. I knew what it was like to have birthdays and Christmases pass by without so much as a card. I knew what it was like to have to get three jobs at age 15 just so I could have food and clothes. I knew what it was like to deal with an alcoholic father beating you until you went numb. I knew what it was like to have a mother so high that she didn't even remember your name. I knew. The more time I spent with the kids, the more I realized that regardless of what the world's standards may be, I was uniquely qualified to deal with these kids in a way that others might not be. I could sense the pain and hurt that many of our kids were dealing with, and I could tell them about the source of my hope. All those painful memories that I had worked so hard to stuff down were the very stories that connected me to the hearts of the kids. In those moments when they are hurting and confused, I can meet them with a message—me too. Then I point them to the source of my hope.

I mentioned my struggle at the beginning of this chapter in the hope that you can relate. Maybe your situation is different, but we have all had disappointments and pain over the course of our lives. I began getting suicide letters from my mom starting at about age 11. I found my father drunk on the side of the road more times than I can remember. I often had to take care of my brother because my parents weren't around. Many of you had problems as a kid too. If we can tap into those places, those hurting places we have left buried under careers and accomplishments and relationships, we can remember what it felt like when we were rejected as kids. Those times where things were not as they should have been. We all have them. Ministering to kids from that place—that real, raw place—will be the moment you step out of the expectation placed on you by people and into the preparation placed on you by God.

2. Kids Are Facing REAL Problems.

We cannot forget the fact that the problems kids face across America are VERY real, and they are getting worse. Here is a short list from just one of our ministry sites this year. This site has about 40 kids on average:

1. A boy got his toe cut off by a family member who was high.
2. A boy was hit by a car and cracked his skull because he was outside alone and went into traffic.
3. A young boy acts out because his 11-year-old brother has cancer.
4. Kids come to church hungry, and we find out that they haven't eaten in three days.
5. We find kids locked outside of their home because their mom isn't done with her happy smoke.
6. Parents are arrested. Too many reasons to list.
7. Kids have never met fathers because they are still in jail.
8. A middle-school-aged boy has not gotten a new pair of shoes in two years because there are 11 kids in his family and they can't afford them.

This is just a sampling of some of the things we learned about in one summer from one group of about 40 kids. Unfortunately, these issues are not unique to our community. And before you think our church must be in a huge city, let me assure you that we are not. We are in a smaller community of about 13,000 people. So, I can guess there are kids in your area that need help too.

GO

3. Kids Are in a REAL Battle.

Many people do not see the importance of reaching outside the four walls of our churches to go and find the lost and hurting kids in our communities. But the enemy does. If you read the list on the previous page, it is undeniable that the enemy has his hands on kids' lives. As adults, we often talk in church about the attack of the enemy, and we can see the traps and pitfalls he is leaving in our path. Yet we forget that the enemy wants to mark us as soon as he can.

Stay alert! Watch out for your great enemy, the devil. He prowls around like a roaring lion, looking for someone to devour.
1 Peter 5:8 (NLT)

Many of us are still fighting battles in our minds that started when we were kids. The same enemy who comes after us comes after them. But there is good news: the same God who redeems us can redeem them. There is a missing link, however. That missing link is you. As believers, we need to realize the importance of fighting for God's kids. My sincere prayer and deep desire are that God would start to open your eyes and heart to the calling He has placed on your life and church.

So many times, I hear from people, even in our own church, that they aren't "called" to outreach ministry. My answer to that is actually not my answer but one we find in Scripture:

Therefore, go and make disciples of all the nations, baptizing them in the name of the Father and the Son and the Holy Spirit.
Matthew 28:19 (NLT)

I believe that when Jesus gave that command, it was to be taken literally. Yet so many of us find ourselves giving excuse after excuse about why *we* aren't the ones He was talking to.

I heard Francis Chan of Cornerstone Church (Simi Valley, CA) give a great analogy about this one time. He was talking about a scenario where he imagined asking his daughter to go and clean her room.

> If I tell my daughter to go clean her room, she knows better than to come back later with her room still messy and say: "I memorized what you said. I can say it in Greek. A group of friends and I are going to get together and study what you said." We need to take Jesus literally and do what He says.[1]

I love this because it so clearly encompasses the attitude some churches take toward outreach ministry. Jesus tells us very clearly to go. He doesn't qualify it. If you are a follower of Jesus and see a need, then that is the only calling you have to experience in order to feel compelled to serve Him in that area. The need IS the call. You already have within you what you need. He has equipped you with your story—your unique and wonderful story that led you to the cross. So take that story, look for a need, and go.

Something to Think About:

What are some things you have experienced in your life that can help you relate to the issues kids are facing? Take some time to reflect on your own past and experience. Is there a place you can identify? Take some time to pray about that right now.

Have you thought about an outreach ministry in your church? Is there already some form of outreach going on that you can build upon? What are some ways you can get outside the four walls of your church? Brainstorm some concrete steps you can take to start reaching out to your community. Sometimes it's about seeing what you have and matching it to a need. Something as simple as leftover soup in a food pantry can be a huge blessing to a new mom who feels isolated. Extra backpacks could be a way to bless a family who is having a hard time making ends meet. Part of the process of deciding

---

[1] Shaffer, Kent. "Francis Chan on Taking Jesus Literally." *Church Relevance*. Share Faith Network, 4 Feb. 2010. Web. 28 Mar. 2017.

GO

where to push forward is looking at what is already in front of you. Ask for ideas from other leaders in your church or ministry of needs they have recognized. Or, figure out a way to engage those in need in what you are already doing. At a conference, I spoke with one children's pastor who was struggling to find a way to start a kids' outreach ministry. Her church, however, ran a program where they provided a hot dog or bratwurst dinner to the neighborhood they were in every Friday. After talking together for a few minutes, she realized how easy it would be to partner with this outreach that was already going on, to bring the element of Sidewalk Sunday school into the parking lot where they served the meal. With some creativity and determination, there are ways to partner with the ministries of most churches in order to include the excluded.

3. WHAT THE WHAT?

As I teach and speak across the country about outreach ministry, many people who want to start their own programs ask the same questions. In this chapter I have listed some of them to give you a broader perspective on the program we run and to help you organize your thoughts as you consider beginning your own.

Q: Can you tell us a little bit about yourself and your church?

A: Currently, I am the Children's and Outreach Pastor at Living Waters Church in Meadville, Pennsylvania. I oversee all programming for children from birth through age twelve. This includes our bus ministry, Sidewalk ministry, Wednesday night programming, and Sunday morning services. Living Waters is unique in our community because our focus is really to seek out the lost who are not currently in a church and bring them Jesus. This goal is evident throughout every area of our ministries. We have a mobile food pantry, evangelism teams that go out into the community, Celebrate Recovery, and Forever Home foster and adoption ministry. We host several community events throughout the year as well. One of the things we focus on as a staff is really getting outside the four walls and ministering to the community.

GO

Q: The main outreach program you run is called Sidewalk Sunday school. What exactly is that? How would you describe it in a sentence or two?

A: In a nutshell, we use the same program that we do on a Sunday morning and take it to the streets. We seek out kids who don't have an opportunity to attend church, and we take church to them.

Q: Do you do this all year long?

A: We are in Pennsylvania, so one of the challenges we have is the weather. The majority of our Sidewalk program runs May through October because those months offer the best opportunity for attendance. We still provide our bus ministry in the off months, as well as host several community events. If you are in an area with a better climate, I would suggest doing the program all year long. We do lose some momentum over the winter, so if you can avoid that, you will be one step ahead.

Q: Why did you decide to start this type of ministry?

A: Most importantly, we started this ministry because Christ commands it. The Bible says we believers are the salt and the light of the earth. Many people stay away from the hardest areas of a community because of crime, drugs, violence, etc. We strive to take the light into the darkness instead of running from it. When we first started our Sidewalk ministry, we targeted the roughest neighborhood in our area. Many people tried to discourage us because of its dangerous environment; however, that is where God called us, and that is why the neighborhood needs Jesus. Yes, there have been challenges, but we have also seen an amazing transformation in the community and in the lives of the people who live there.

Secondly, some kids will *never* hear the gospel otherwise. I never can quite comprehend this, but at every site, every year, we find kids who have never heard the gospel before. These kids are growing up in situations where the enemy most certainly has his hands on them. Our responsibility is to share the truth of the gospel with them. The first step to any kind of lasting change in their situation is Jesus.

Q: How effective is this type of ministry?

A: It's very effective. When we send out a church bus on Sunday mornings, we bring in about 60 kids at most from the neighborhood. When we go into the community, however, we see close to 200 kids. Therefore, if we are taking the gospel to them instead of bringing them to us, we can reach more kids. Now that we have been in the neighborhoods for several years, we are seeing how this ministry not only impacts the kids but the entire family. This impact is a direct result of an encounter with Jesus.

Q: How would you describe the kids you are reaching? We know each child is unique, but give us a feel for the type of kids you're reaching out to. What types of homes do they come from? What is their background? What are their neighborhoods like?

A: This is a heartbreaking question to answer. In the church, we often support missions' trips. I go on them myself, and they have been life changing, so don't get me wrong. But what we often don't realize is that there are kids in need right in our own backyards. The kids we reach through Sidewalk ministry are lost. Many are unsupervised, even as young as toddlers. It's normal to go down into a neighborhood

GO

and find kids all over the place with no adults around. They often have no food to eat, and parents are either high or looking for the best way to achieve their next high. The kids have clothes and shoes that are in terrible condition or do not fit. Their teeth are rotting out. They are lucky if they have a bed, and if they do, chances are they have to share it with at least one other person. The reality is that many of these kids are hungry. They are thirsty. They need clothes. They need attention. They need Jesus. And there are kids like this in most communities across the country.

Many times people tell me that what we are doing isn't necessary because government organizations take care of these kids. They claim there are programs already doing what we are doing. Unfortunately, there is a disconnect between the way these organizations should be operating and in what they actually do. The bottom line is that these kids are not having their needs met by government programs. Whether it is lack of accountability, a faulty system, or something else, all the kids at our sites have similar struggles. It's a widespread problem. Recently, we were in one neighborhood where the homes have broken windows, no steps, no furniture, and are filthy. One of our volunteers was going to skip over a house because he thought no one could possibly be living there. I knocked on the door, and there were five children inside. Many of these families are one step away from homelessness or having their kids taken from them. It is heartbreaking. But you know what? Kids are kids, and Jesus is Jesus.

Sometimes people think it is too hard to connect with these kids, but what we quickly realize is that they are starved for attention and affection. Once you start meeting those emotional needs, as well as the physical needs, you can very easily meet the spiritual needs. I would say the majority of the kids we have met have given their hearts to the Lord. In the first three weeks of our ministry, we saw over 150 kids respond to the gospel message. These are first time decisions for

GO

Christ—many of the kids hearing the gospel for the very first time. To me, this is a mission field. No passport required. And this is not something that other "agencies" are doing. They are treating the symptoms instead of the problem, and that simply isn't working. We have families that have been living in poverty for generations. The hope for change comes from a relationship with Jesus.

Q: Let's get more into the details of how Sidewalk Sunday school works. How do you get the word out that you're there?

A: Recently, we started a new ministry site in a trailer park where we had very little previous contact, and I knew it would be a challenge. In many of the other sites we started, we already had contact with a couple of kids from our bus ministry. This time we knew we were going to have to be creative in how we marketed the program and let people know about it.

We had gotten the park manager's permission ahead of time to be there. Then we downloaded the "ice cream truck" song from iTunes and played it from our mobile ministry truck. When kids came out to see the ice cream truck, we gave them FREE ice cream sandwiches. The news quickly spread, and soon kids were everywhere. Along with the ice cream, we handed out flyers with information about when and where we would be meeting. We had a couple of our teens dressed up in full body costumes just to give the kids attention.

We were allowed to have meetings in a grassy area, and the kids were SO hungry for the Word. We had close to 100% attendance of the kids who lived in that neighborhood—an incredible turn out for a new site. Since the launch, that site has really taken root, and we have a sense of permanency with our program at that location now.

GO

Q: How long is a typical program?

A: The main program lasts about an hour. We keep it fast paced because that's what kids need. We are competing for time with the "X-Box generation," as I call them. You have to make the program exciting and fun. In that hour, we are constantly changing what we do and how we do it in order to keep the kids' attention. We do spend a little more time at each site after the program is over, just praying and talking with the kids. I would allow about two hours total for the complete program.

Q: Let's talk about some of the individual components of each program. What types of games work with a crowd like this? Can you suggest games for large groups that don't require a whole lot of explanation?

A: As an example, something fun that we do is a simple hula hoop tournament. Games are always Boys vs. Girls—it adds to the excitement. Round 1 is 3 girls against 3 boys. Whoever hula hoops the longest wins that round. Then we have the winning girl and winning boy go against each other for Round 2, but Round 2 requires them to walk while hooping to another adult about 50 feet away. Whoever gets there first wins 1000 points. On Round 3 we have them start hooping, and then unwrap and eat an ice cream sandwich while hooping. Whoever finishes first wins 2000 points. We keep track of all the points throughout the games, as it adds an extra element of excitement for the kids and motivates them to participate. The winner of the hula hoop games gets a prize. Prizes are anything from candy to a can of pop, or puzzles and books.

You can use pretty much any game for the program. We usually ask review questions from the week before, and only pick kids to participate who can correctly answer the questions. This is another added incentive to keep them engaged and paying attention. We use a lot of large group games, games that you would play at camp, etc. Some of the games have to be modified, depending on location. At some sites we have a grassy field to play in. At other sites, we are on a small section of concrete, so it requires some creative thinking. The key here is to keep the kids guessing and always have something different. One week we might be catching goldfish out of a tank, the next week it might be a watermelon eating contest, the next week it might be a pie in the face of a popular volunteer. Games are one of the things that keep the kids coming back.

Q: Why do you use candy and prizes? Isn't that like bribery?

A: Sometimes I have people criticize me for giving away prizes or candy. Here are my thoughts on that. If a Blow Pop or an ice cream cone can get kids to come and stay with me for an hour so I can give them the gospel, that treat grants me the opportunity to develop a relationship with them. Those things aren't the focus—they are the tools we use to draw kids in. Once you have relationships, you can cut back on that stuff, but in the beginning it's hard to get the kids without it. It's really no different than serving coffee in church to the adults.

When first starting out, leaders need to establish authority. Many of these kids have not had good boundaries established for them, and they have to be taught an element of respect. Without that, you can't teach them, so being consistent and following through is imperative. Many times, having the ability to use prizes as a tool to manage behavior will be enough to get the kids to listen. I realize some people may have an issue with that, but my mentality is that we need to

GO

do whatever it takes to reach these kids. If "whatever" means giving them bubble gum afterwards, then I'm okay with that.

Q: What do you do for worship? What works well in this setting?

A: I always start small with worship time, doing something simple and high energy. A favorite is a Hillsong Kids' song, "Jesus Is My Superhero." It has motions you can teach the kids, and they love it. Gradually, we add another song or two. I also like to use JUMPSTART3 (http://jumpstart3.com) because the worship songs are upbeat and fun, with Scripture as the lyrics. This gets the Word into the kids' hearts and minds in a way that really captures their attention. There are also motions kids can do, which will help them remember. We recently added the Yancy version of "How Great Is Our God" with motions. It is easy for the kids to learn and helps them worship. We go right from that song into a prayer for the program, and that settles the kids down. It is amazing to watch a group of kids on the street with their eyes closed, hands raised, singing about how great our God is. There's nothing else like it.

Q: How many people does it take to do one program? How do you get volunteers?

A: If we have to, my husband and I can lead the program alone, especially if we know the kids in the neighborhood, but it works best when we have a team. In the beginning, volunteers were more difficult to find because no one had any idea what I was talking about—they had nothing to compare this ministry to. But when people start seeing and hearing about what God is doing, they want to get involved. Initially, we only did two sites—now we have eight. With the amount of time and attention each site takes, it would be impossible for me to do all of that by myself, so now we operate in teams. Each team has about four or five people; most are there consistently each week. It's not hard to get volunteers once they start hearing and seeing the testimonies. People want to be involved where they know God is working and moving.

Q: What types of volunteers do you look for? Are there specific roles on each team that you're trying to fill?

A: Actually, leadership skills are not what I look for. I look for a servant's heart. A teachable spirit and a heart for kids are way more important than talent. Someone who is living a spirit led life will easily be touched by this ministry, and God will use them when they step out in obedience to the call. We see it happen all the time. 90% is showing up, and God just does the rest. Right now, one of my most effective volunteers is an older retired man who only volunteered to drive the truck but quickly started developing relationships with the kids. God is using him in a way he never imagined.

With regard to roles, ideally we want people serving in an area that works for them. Our church offers a class where we look at each individual's personality, spiritual gifts, and passions. In the center of those three, you can find your purpose. Once we examine that, we can easily see where a person might be the best fit. For some, it might be worship or prayer. For others, it might be leading games, serving food, or teaching. Our goal, even as a church, is to let people serve where God has uniquely equipped them. Then they will be serving as an outpouring of their heart. Our pastor often says that you don't get burned out doing *a lot* of a thing.... You get burned out from doing the *wrong* things. We don't want anyone burned out. We want them serving in a way that they are not only being obedient to what God

GO

has called them to do, but in a way that ignites that fire inside of them. Once you find that sweet spot, you can't stop them.

Q: How many sites do you visit and how often do you go out?

A: Each year looks a little bit different. We have had up to eight sites. We go out weekly to each site for the program, and then each team has a visitation schedule so the kids get visited at least once in between sessions. Our goal is to increase the number of sites each year until we are reaching as far into our community as we can. The foundation of this ministry is relationships, and those are created more through visitation than through the Sidewalk session. Building relationships is an imperative part of the ministry.

Q: How do visitations work? What else do you do to follow up with these kids?

A: We visit the homes of the kids that attended the program that week. We have an attendance form that has the kids' addresses on it, and we use it to keep track of where the kids live. Early in the season, we blitz the whole neighborhood and go door to door with flyers. We also visit the neighborhood to just hang out with whoever is outside. I take popsicles, apples, etc. and just play with the kids. That's actually when a lot of ministry happens—in those informal moments where kids and parents learn to trust you.

Q: What advice would you give someone who is thinking about starting this type of ministry?

A: First of all, start praying about locations in your community that need this ministry. Look for low-income housing, apartment complexes, trailer parks, etc. Pray for open doors, open hearts, and favor with the Father. Don't get too intimidated to start. Just start small and go from there. The most important thing is to get off the bench and do something. Each site will be a little bit different, and that's okay. Just start some sort of program for the kids. We have a truck now, but we began with my minivan. This is one of the most rewarding ministries and will change your heart forever. I promise!

Q: If people want more information or have questions, how can they contact you?

A: You can email me at rachael@livingwaterschurch.tv, or find me on Facebook. I would be happy to help anyone get started.

Q: Do you have anything else to add?

A: One thing I always tell people is that even though it is good to ask questions and do research, your experience is going to be different than mine, just like each church is a little bit different. The most important thing is to make a plan and then follow through. Don't keep talking about going—just go.

4. LOVE KIDS— LOVE THEIR FAMILIES

On top of the white board in my office is a clear clip that is meant to hold a thin dry erase marker. Instead, it holds a bullet. I keep it there as a reminder of what God has done in the last couple of years.

When I first met Eli, he was about 10 years old. He was one of the kids you could always find outside, no matter the time of day or the weather. During the first year in one of our neighborhoods, I intentionally visit every couple of days, even if I just drive through and talk to the kids who are outside. On one of those unplanned visits, I met this smart kid as he was walking along the street. He recognized me from Sidewalk, even though he hadn't come yet. He had watched from a distance, he told me, but thought he was too old. As I asked him some questions about school, I realized he was much older than he appeared. He was small for his age, as many of our kids are, due to lack of good nutrition. He had a younger brother who overshadowed him in height by at least a foot. Because of this, it was easy initially to lump him into the "little kid" category when you had a big group.

During our impromptu meetings outside, I started to learn who Eli was, what he liked to do, and how one of the things he was really craving was conversation. He had so many stories for me, most of which weren't true, but over time, some truth started to trickle out. He and the kids were alone a lot. He had to take care of siblings a lot.

GO

He was scared a lot. As he began to trust me, I started to see in him what I see in so many kids we work with. Eli, even though he was known at school as a troublemaker, was actually a great kid inside. He was groomed by his environment to fall into that category because kids aren't supposed to raise themselves. Kids aren't supposed to have to parent. God designed kids to need nurturing and love, and when children don't receive those things, especially for a long time, they only exhibit what they have experienced.

As we were talking one day, Eli told me that he had something for me. I was used to the little kids bringing me gifts but not the older ones. As he held out his hand, I looked down to see a dull gray bullet. It was pretty large and scraped up.

"Where did you get this?" I asked.

He answered me quietly. "One of the cops that was down here last night dropped it."

As he said those words, I just looked down at his hand, not knowing what to say. He told me that the night before there were six cop cars and lots of shouting near his home. He was outside when it happened, but he ran into the woods behind his apartment to hide until it was over. He wasn't sure whom, but someone had been taken away in a police car. As he walked back to his house, he realized his dad was the one who had been taken away. While he was trying to figure out exactly what had happened, he stepped on something. He looked down to find a stray bullet that had somehow fallen out of the gun one of the police officers had used. Now, here in his hand, this bullet was being offered to me as a gift. I struggled to make sense of where his mind was going.

"We need hope down here," he said, with tears in his eyes. "That's what you do."

As I graciously accepted his gift, I prayed for the right words to say. I had never been up against such a huge task in my life. I didn't feel like I was even qualified to measure up to such a challenge. I didn't begin to understand the extent of what the kids in this neighborhood were going through, and I felt like I was in over my head. In that moment, however, the Holy Spirit reminded me that even though I did not know what I was doing, HE did.

For the Holy Spirit will teach you at that time what needs to be said.
Luke 12:12 (NLT)

I honestly don't remember what I said that day. I do remember hugging Eli, praying with him, crying with him, and explaining to him that no matter what, God would never leave him.

One of the biggest reasons people give me for not doing outreach is that they do not feel qualified to meet the heavy needs that this type of ministry can bring. I agree that it can be overwhelming at times. But I also know that if you are a believer in the Lord Jesus Christ, if you have surrendered your heart and life to Him, then you have access to ALL of Him, not just part of Him. That means that as a disciple, when you are "in the trenches" and you come upon a mess, you have access to the wisdom, boldness, strength, and words of the Holy Spirit. If we position ourselves as vessels—as willing servants—then realistically, the Holy Spirit's role is to minister to those He brings into our paths. If we don't know what to say, what to do, or how to act, that's okay. Yes, it's okay. Because He does. He knew exactly the words Eli needed to hear that day, and He knows exactly the words that need to be shared in your situation too. Don't get so caught up in what might happen that you lose sight of what has already happened. The finished work on the cross has already given followers of Jesus access to what we need to carry out this task.

I continued to keep a close eye on Eli, and the following week he came to Sidewalk. But this time, instead of one brother, he brought along all of his siblings—all five of them. As we watched, all six of those

GO

kids came to faith in Christ through our consistent Sidewalk efforts. It was incredible to witness what God was doing. Every week we would also send home information about our bus that picks families up on Sundays for church. Eli told me that he had been praying for his mom to come. I joined him in that prayer and watched each week as the bus arrived at the church. About three weeks later, I was pleasantly surprised to see Eli proudly escorting his mom through the doors of the church. As he did, I gave him the thumbs-up sign. He showed her around with such pride, and his attitude and actions matched his age. I prayed the entire service as I was teaching in the kids' class. I couldn't leave to see if Eli's mom was still in service or if she was responding to the message. As I grew a little anxious, God reminded me that it was His plan to get her there in the first place and that I just needed to trust Him. As I relaxed a little bit, I thanked Him for pursuing us, even when we don't want to be pursued. And I thanked Him for using Eli.

After church, Eli's mom joined him on the bus and they left. Later that week I learned that his mom, Amber, had decided to give her life to Christ at the altar that Sunday morning. As I heard the news, I realized the Sidewalk ministry we are doing is not just about the kids—it is about families. The following Sunday Amber came back. She started to come consistently with the kids, and I could see things in her life start to change. Eventually, Eli's dad, Anthony, got out of jail and joined Amber on the bus. The very first morning that he came to church, he also gave his heart to the Lord. In a period of less than two months, we saw an entire family—mom, dad, and six children—come to faith in Christ. God had used our Sidewalk ministry to impact an entire family.

As we started to invest in this family, we learned that Eli's mom and dad were not actually married, neither had jobs, and they had no vehicle. We started getting them plugged in to Bible studies and life

GO

groups. We sent people to walk alongside them, and we started to see incredible changes in their life. Within a short time, both of them got full time jobs and were able to purchase a used car. They no longer had to ride the bus, but came on their own to church.

On one of the first couple of Sundays that they came on their own, the message was one that referenced God's plan for marriage. After the message, Anthony made his way up to speak with our senior pastor. "That thing you were talking about—about having sex before marriage? Well, we do that...a lot. I think we better get married." Oh my word. The pastor stammered a bit as he gathered his words, and the 93-year-old woman who was sitting within earshot had never opened her eyes so wide in her life. But you know what? The following month, on Valentines Day, we had the privilege of being involved in our first Sidewalk Sunday school wedding. And it was incredible. This family had been completely transformed within a few short months, and it was such an honor and privilege to be part of that wedding. Since that time, the family has moved away because Anthony was offered a good job in another town. Occasionally, they visit and bring the kids to see us. They still have some struggles, as is the case with most families, but the path they are on now is completely different than the one we found them on.

That's the gospel. That's why we do what we do. That's why we need to get outside the four walls of our church and go find people who need Jesus. They aren't going to wander into our churches on their own. Lost people are just that...lost.

For the Son of Man came to seek and save those who are lost.
Luke 19:10 (NLT)

As we pattern our ministry after Jesus', let's not forget that "seek" part.

. . .

GO

"What's wrong with your head?" I asked. I was holding one of my little friends on my lap, and we were sharing a snack of cookies and juice boxes.

"Nothing," he said.

"Look at me," I demanded. As he did, I could see the tears welling up in his eyes. "What happened?" I asked again softly.

"My mom banged my head against the concrete."

I sighed heavily. It angered me to think that this precious little one had been mistreated. Instantly, I started to think of all the things I wanted to say to his mother. I simply could not explain to this little one why or how this had happened to him. I made a mental list of agencies I needed to call, and I immediately judged this mom as a bad mom.

Confronting abuse is one of the hardest areas of this type of ministry. We see so many hard things in the lives of these kids that it is very easy to become calloused towards the parents. The protective mama bear in me started to become enraged at the thought of this little one and how he must have felt as the incident happened—confused, hurt, angry, sad. I was too. As I prayed for him and taught him how to pray for healing, I noticed some of the other kids were watching for my reaction. I remained calm even though I was reeling inside. I sensed they were looking to see if I was someone safe that they could share their own stories with. I reminded my little friend how much I loved him, how much God loved him, and I held him a little tighter. As I continued to think about his mom, however, the Lord intercepted my thoughts.

"I love her."

What?

"I love her," the Holy Spirit whispered. "I love her, and I died for her too."

Wow. I did not see that coming. I felt I had some "righteous anger" toward her and that He would agree with me. But as much as I am sure that God was grieved by the actions this mom took toward this little boy, that is not what God spoke to me that day. Instead, He spoke love. This was so contrary to what I was feeling and thinking that I absolutely *know* it had to come from the Holy Spirit. I wanted to be angry and fight for this little boy; instead, God had another plan at that moment.

Now, before you send me an email, I want you to know that I did report the incident to the appropriate agencies. But I did not lash out at that mom. Instead, I decided to do a little research on substance abuse, which I knew was a struggle the mom was dealing with. As I did, I learned some things that have been very important in how we minister to families on the street.

First, there is a difference between substance abuse and addiction. Before this incident, I had kind of lumped them into the same category. I think most of the church does. It makes it easier to justify our judgment. Substance abuse is something that is rampant in the lives of many people, including people in the church. Typically, it starts out as a painkiller for a toothache or a beer after a hard day. What starts out innocently for most people becomes substance abuse when they start using the substance more often and more intensely than they should. The toothache is gone, but that painkiller will also help with the pain of rejection. That cold one with the guys becomes two, or three, or six because it helps sleep to come after a stressful day. At this point, many people could still get a grip and choose to stop if they wanted, but it's a slippery slope.

At last, the point comes where substance abuse becomes full-fledged addiction. Painkillers are replaced by heroin once the prescriptions run out. Alcohol to help induce sleep becomes a crutch just to get through the day. Something happens in the brain when addiction takes over. The chemical craving in the body is so consuming that

GO

rational thoughts, decisions, and actions become irrelevant. It's not until after that next hit, next drink, or next release of chemicals in the brain that anything else can even occupy thoughts. *Anything* else. Including children. When a parent is struggling with full blown addiction, much of what they do, or don't do, is so clouded by the object of their addiction that the child is not even seen or heard over the chemical cravings going on inside the body. Then what? How are they able to master their addiction? Even if lucid thoughts come and go, how are they to get to a treatment center if they ask for help? If they admit to anyone that they are struggling, their children will be taken from them, yet they can't continue to parent in the state they are in.

I believe the role of the church should be to come alongside these parents and help point them toward recovery. Now, I am not saying this is completely necessary before you start your Sidewalk ministry. But very early on, as you start to get involved in the lives of the kids, you will realize there is a huge need in our culture for the church to start helping these people walk toward freedom. Be aware and pray for opportunities to start linking struggling parents with those who have walked this road and come out on the other side.

Once I gained this perspective, I realized that coming alongside this family in love and support was going to have a much more lasting impact than yelling at the mom about what she had done to her little boy. If we can come to a place where we minister the way Jesus did…with love…we will see that it's not our angry words that change someone. It's Jesus who changes someone.

As You Begin Your Outreach Ministry

Our goal is always to make a lasting difference in the life of a child. That happens not just with salvation but with discipleship. As you start to impact children, you realize that the children will reach their parents. In order to have a successful outreach to the parents, you need to have a plan in place to help get them plugged in and supported. Ultimately, this should be the goal of every church—not just to preach salvation but to make disciples.

> *Therefore, go and make disciples of all the nations, baptizing them in the name of the Father and the Son and the Holy Spirit.*
> Matthew 28:19 (NLT)

Notice that Jesus does not tell us to make converts; He tells us to make disciples. How can we do that with families from hard places? By offering a safety net to catch them when they fall. It took us a while to get the hang of this, and we are still learning as we go, but I believe it is necessary in order to offer families the chance at transformation that comes when they become fully committed followers of Christ.

Something to Think About:

Here is a list of things to consider as you start your outreach ministry.

1. Women's Ministry: Talk to your women's ministry director about what you are planning on doing. If you do not have a women's ministry director, than talk to a pastor's wife, an elder's wife, or even just a wise woman who has a heart for the Lord. Explain to her your heart for reaching families and how that may impact your church. Ask her to start praying along with you for the women you will be meeting and ways the women's ministry can join you in reaching out. As you start ministering in these communities, you will realize how many needs there are that the body of Christ can help with. Sharing some of the testimonies with a heart of compassion will start to cast vision on those who have a heart to help. Once I started sharing some of the situations we encountered on the street, there quickly became an apparent desire for women to help. These stay-at-home moms, grandmas, and women in general have the resources, time, and talents we need. They are the perfect choice to get the people you

GO

are reaching out to in the community plugged in to some relationships in the church. Some things we do include: sending meals when a mom has a baby, a card ministry for encouragement, rides to women's Bible study, Mother's Day gifts, babysitting help, sending along a few women to minister on-site to the moms during Sidewalk, mentorship, making Christmas stockings, helping purchase school supplies or snack supplies, etc.

What we have found is that many of the women in our church have a desire to reach out to the lost and hurting in our community. The disconnect is that they simply don't know what the needs are. One of your roles will be acting as a champion for the kids you are ministering to. Presenting the needs and reaching out to those in your church who are willing to meet the needs is a key connection point in an effective Sidewalk ministry. I cannot even express to you how much it changes a mom's heart when she has received an unexpected blessing from someone in the church. We have seen moms who have been hardened and closed off to church and God become immersed in a culture of love and acceptance. That in turn, leads them to a place where they can truly "feel" what the love of Christ is like as He draws them to Himself. Their salvation is then supported and discipleship can happen in a much more natural way, through relationships and consistency.

2. Men's Ministry: A men's ministry offers the valuable resource of men with skills who may also have the desire to help out in other areas. Many of the retired men in our church are at a place in life where they would gladly help out if they knew of the need. A great thing to keep in mind is that many men are task oriented, so when asking the men's group for help, it's best to go with specific requests. Even if the request is for prayer, be specific. Ask a specific man to pray for a specific request for a specific child or family. Also, invite men

to do helpful tasks like teaching a child to change a chain on his/her bike, change a tire, play football, etc. Another way to get men involved is to have a team of guys available to help families move. What we have seen over the last couple of years is that as families are transformed by the gospel, they make positive changes in their lives, which enable them to leave the neighborhoods we found them in. Having a practical ministry of fixing things, moving things, and the like is a great way for men to connect to the kids' ministry that is happening on the street.

3. Life Group or Recovery Group: If your church has a recovery group, you will want to get well acquainted with the leader. What we often see is that there are many parents who feel trapped in their current situation. Getting them connected with a support group that addresses their area of need can be essential in helping them become healthy mentally, physically, or spiritually. Even if they are going to formal meetings like AA, the relationships with those who have come out of addiction can be so valuable in helping them avoid slipping as they walk out of that lifestyle. Recovery is a process, and even though you may be called to work with kids, you will inevitably become involved with the parents as you get to know and love families. Having life and recovery groups to point them to is a great resource.

4. Hospitality Group: We have an entire lunch team that prepares a bagged lunch for our kids at every site. Initially, I was making hundreds of lunches each week. What I realized was that there are people in our church who truly have the gift of hospitality. They *enjoy* making all those lunches. I don't. I enjoy knowing my kids have full bellies and can listen and learn, but I don't enjoy making hundreds of sandwiches every week. Our dedicated team works together, and even includes some people who cannot serve in other areas due to physical

GO

or mental limitations. Including them in serving God's kids helps them feel connected in such a way that food preparation becomes a ministry in and of itself. I have one lady who prays over every single meal that is prepared. That is so encouraging to me! Something as simple as a peanut butter and jelly sandwich can be a source of blessing to a child because of the prayers that have gone into it. Finding these types of people in your church can help lighten your load, as well as help people serve with the gifts God has given them.

5. Prayer Group: Even though this group is last on this list, don't think for one second that it is the least important. In fact, it's the *most* important. Without prayer, your ministry will fail. Period. Regardless of how great a teacher you may be and how dedicated and passionate you are, your ministry simply will not work without prayer. You need prayer for wisdom and to be able to hear from God the direction He wants you to take with His kids. Your helpers need prayer in order to be able to sustain hope when faced with the type of issues the kids you work with face. Your kids need prayer for safety and for their hearts to be opened so they can receive what you are trying to teach them. The communities you are working in need prayer, as many times you are going into dark places. Your church needs prayer as the families start to trickle in, and they look different, smell different, talk different, and act different than people who grew up in church. Your leadership needs prayer, as this type of ministry will inevitably bring challenges as the church starts to grow as a result of families getting connected. This entire ministry simply has to be bathed in prayer. What I suggest is starting by asking for general prayers. Then get specific as needs are laid on your heart. I have multiple people I can call at any given moment for prayer. You will be up against some things that you are not prepared for. I mention many of mine in this book, and there are more every week. Just when I think I have seen and heard it

all, it becomes apparent that I haven't. Reconciling those emotions as a leader and navigating those hard waters is impossible without prayer. Be intentional about setting yourself up with a network of prayer warriors—the kind that stop and pray when you ask them, not the kind that say they will and forget. You know the people I am talking about; God is already bringing some prayer warriors to mind, isn't He? Stop what you are doing right now and call them. They need to be covering you in prayer as you seek God for how to get this ministry started.

As I have listed a few areas to consider here, I want to mention one more thing. Don't get overwhelmed. So many times I talk with people at conferences or on the phone, and they feel intimidated to get started. Don't let that happen to you. I always say that 90% of this ministry is just showing up. God will show you the next step. After all, isn't that exactly what faith is? Stepping out in obedience even if you don't know God's whole plan? Start small; start simple. The important thing is just to go.

5. LESSONS IN GRACE

Very few kids in my life have made me want to quit. Typically, I am able to separate the child from the behavior and work through the issues until we see progress. I usually go after the kids no one else wants to work with and stay with them until everyone wants to work with them. However, very early in our Sidewalk ministry days, I met my match in Cameron, a little boy who was desperate for some attention and showed it by acting out constantly. Initially, he would come to Sidewalk maybe to get some candy or to follow his friends, but mostly to start trouble. He generally would wander in for the game and slip out before the lesson. As a result, it was very hard for me to reach him because he didn't stick around for long. As much as I had hoped to connect with him, I also had a group of kids sitting in front of me who needed my time and attention. I watched as he came and went, week after week, and I found myself praying about him often.

On one particularly sunny Sunday, I was out greeting the kids as they got off the bus. Within a matter of seconds, Cameron jumped past me and ran into the building. Following quickly after him, I realized he had taken an entire box of Pop-Tarts that I had out for the kids, and was hiding in the arcade with them. On Sundays, we meet in a movie theater because we have outgrown our building, so the arcade is a huge distraction to most of the boys. My husband, who is wonderful with the hardest of kids, was able to get him to come into the classroom, but it was all we could do to keep him there. As

GO

I was teaching our lesson, I watched Cameron bounce around the room while our loyal volunteers tried to corral him. Realistically, I'm not sure there was a whole lot they could do. He really did the opposite of anything anyone asked of him. Participating in the lesson, or even sitting, was proving to be impossible for this little guy. In fact, when the time came for a serious moment where kids were getting ready to pray for salvation, Cameron very loudly and very distractingly started hitting other kids and arguing with them. It almost felt as if he were intentionally trying to derail everything I was working so hard to do.

This type of scenario continued week after week. I was determined to find something that worked, so I started to pull out some of my "teacher" tricks. I used prizes, rewards, stern looks, quiet seat games—you name it. One day, toward the end of a particularly hard morning with him, I admitted to myself that I couldn't handle him. As he left on the bus, I sat down in defeat. Thoughts of giving up ran through my mind. "I can't do this. I'm not trained for this. I don't know how to deal with kids like this. I'm not cut out for this." My husband, always perceptive of my mood and the temperature of the classroom, recognized my feelings of failure and just looked at me. I could feel his eyes on me and knew he wanted to say something, but he didn't. He busied himself, cleaned up our supplies, and led me to the car. As we drove home, I noticed he did not take the typical route. Instead, he turned into the neighborhood Cameron lived in. "I don't want to come here!" I immediately argued. My husband remained silent and then pulled up behind our church bus that was just dropping the kids off. As I watched Cameron get off the bus, I was suddenly overcome with what I can only describe as a moment from the Holy Spirit. I called out to Cameron. He turned around and was surprised to see me.

"Cameron, I just want to tell you that I love you," I said.

GO

After the shock ran off his face, the hugest smile I've ever seen came over him. "I love you too, Ms. Rachael," he confessed. Then he turned around and walked home.

As we pulled away, I glanced over at my husband. He drove confidently home, a quiet smile on his face. "Thank you. That was exactly what I needed," I conceded.

At the time, I knew something changed for Cameron and me that day, though I couldn't explain what it was. It was a turning point for us. I now know it was the beginning of a relationship that was going to be forged out of repeated conversations and visits—a relationship that was not just teacher/student, but one of friendship. I started to feel and think differently about him as I prayed consistently for him. I didn't know much about his home life, but I knew that living where he did, his life would be complicated. It was a hard neighborhood. I decided I would be intentional about learning more about him and trying to figure out how to reach him.

The following Sunday, my husband was teaching, and I could feel the frustration dripping from his words. Cameron was treating him much the same way he treated me. As I tried to help with the game we were playing, I realized I was going to have to deal with Cameron if the class was going to get anything done that day. He was so distracting that the rest of the kids were being robbed of time and attention. In the past, if something like this came up, we typically would ask parents to have a conversation with their child. For the kids coming in on the bus, however, that wasn't an option. I decided to ask him to sit with me on the movie theater steps, and I simply asked him how his week went. As we sat, I listened to Cameron talk. And talk. And TALK! He talked about Spider-Man, he talked about football, he talked about his sweatshirt, he talked about bugs, he talked about his teacher at school.... The kid would not stop talking. I picked up rather quickly that this little guy was simply looking for someone to talk to.

GO

Most of my frustrations with him had stemmed from him wanting to talk and me wanting him to be quiet. Instead of looking at what his needs really were, I ignored them in order to meet the needs I thought he had. It wasn't intentional; it was inexperience. Just like the need to be fed, kids have a need to be heard. For whatever reason, Cameron needed me to listen. We chatted for quite a while, and I could see a change coming over him. He eventually got to a place of pause—I'm not sure even he knew why—but I think he got to the place where he felt heard. The Lord had quieted his heart, just enough, that it opened up an opportunity for me to speak the words the Lord had used to speak to me. I leaned over, whispered something loud enough for only him to hear, and then we both went back to participating in the game. From that point on, the rest of the morning went smoothly. Cameron was engaged, he listened, he responded. He actually prayed for salvation at the end of that lesson. The difference we could see in such a short amount of time was remarkable.

As we cleaned up that day, my husband asked me what I had whispered to Cameron because it had obviously been effective. "I told him he was my favorite," I explained. Content with that answer, my husband nodded in agreement. I realized the main ingredient that Cameron was missing in our classroom was one-on-one attention and time from a caring adult. I have seen this pattern over and over as we have worked with kids in our Sidewalk program during the last couple of years. Sometimes, the hardest kids are the ones who need love the most.

Four years later, as I look at who Cameron is today, it is almost impossible to recognize him as the same kid. Now, he is one of my biggest assets in the children's department. Though he is still technically young enough to be in my class, he has become one of the best helpers I have. He is more dedicated and hard working than some of my adult volunteers. This transition has not been an easy one, but it

GO

was a necessary one. It took time. It took us investing in and spending time with him. It took countless hours of talking and listening. It took consistent and confident prayers. It took dedication to seeing him through, celebrating his victories, and comforting his losses. Some days were better than others. He still holds the record for getting kicked out of class the most times; however, every single frustrating moment has been worth it.

One day, after we had finished a lesson, Cameron came to me with a very hard question. "Ms. Rachael, what would happen to my mom if she died and didn't know about Jesus?"

I took a deep breath and prayed a quick prayer before answering. "Well, Cameron, the Bible says that we come to faith in Christ by believing in Jesus. That's how we get to spend eternity with God."

He watched me intently as I explained once again God's plan for salvation. He had tears in his eyes and was without words, which was rare for him. He finally started to respond, almost a little panicky, "I have to go home right now and tell them—my whole family. If I don't tell them, they won't know."

I explained to him that he would need to wait until service was over for the bus to take him back home, but I prayed with him for his family, right then and there. This was a pivotal moment for him because he finally and completely understood the message of the gospel. He calmed a little but paced the hall until it was time to leave. I hugged him as he left, and I told him I would be praying for his conversation with his parents.

Later that week, I dropped by his house to see him, but he wasn't home. I tried once or twice more throughout the week, but each time he wasn't there. So Sunday morning, I waited anxiously by the door as he got off the bus. As he did, a cute little redhead hopped off the bus behind him. All he said was, "This is my sister." I noticed a hint of disgust—not the kind that means you really have disgust for someone, rather the kind you show for an annoying sibling who is currently driving you crazy.

"Cameron!" I exclaimed. "You brought your sister! I didn't even know you had a sister!" I was so excited.

"My mom says she will come next week," he grudgingly replied.

As they got situated in class, I pulled Cameron aside and asked him how his conversation went with his family. He explained that he had told them everything he knew, but he wasn't sure if they heard or understood him. I promised to keep praying for Cameron's family.

Since that time, we have been so excited to watch Cameron's entire family become part of our church family. One-by-one, they have all come to faith in Christ. Mom, dad, and three other kids are all walking with Jesus as a direct result of Cameron being bold enough to share his faith with his family. I know many adults who do not have that boldness or see those results. I am so thankful I did not give up on Cameron when I felt like I was getting nowhere. His entire family now loves and serves God.

This past summer, I had the awesome privilege of baptizing Cameron. I have never had a prouder moment in my career as a minister of the gospel than the moment I witnessed Cameron publicly proclaim his faith in Christ. The road we have traveled together has been an incredible journey. I am so excited to see how God will continue to use Cameron.

Kids with Hard Backgrounds

In our ministry—especially since starting to do outreach on a regular basis—we often have to deal with challenging kids. This is not to be unexpected when you work with kids from hard places. Many of the kids in the neighborhoods we work in have faced some sort of traumatic situation. Working with kids who have traumatic backgrounds can be very difficult, especially if you are inexperienced. Although I had much experience with kids, they were typically "churched" kids who were brought to us by their parents. Rarely does that happen in Sidewalk or bus ministry—most of the time kids come on their own.

I have found that the key to successfully working with the hardest kids is relationship. I know building relationships takes a lot of work and time. I *know* it does. But it is time well spent. Going to a basketball game or eating an ice cream cone together can be important tools to unlocking the heart of a child. Consistency is key. Showing up when you say you are going to show up, and even showing up when you aren't expected, is imperative to forging a relationship that lasts with a kid. Once you have the relationship, formed by giving consistent, intentional time, you have earned the right to speak into kids' lives. This takes sacrifice; however, once the relationship is established, you will find that the need to discipline decreases significantly. This was evident as I worked with Cameron. Now, I am not saying that today Cameron is perfect for every teacher. In fact, the opposite is true. If I am not in the classroom, he will test and try each teacher until he gets to know him or her. But with me, it's different. Our relationship makes it different. I've invested so much into him that he knows I love him, and he naturally wants me to be proud of him.

Church in Transition

When we first started bringing kids to church on the bus from our Sidewalk sites, our church family took a little bit of time to transition. I want to be open about this because this may happen at your church as well. Even if you are not doing a bus ministry, hopefully some of the families from your outreaches will make their way into your church. As that happens, one thing needs to be on the hearts of the people in your church who will be serving them—grace. I'm going to repeat that so you hear me: grace, grace, GRACE! The kids or families who come in may not look or act like what you are used to

GO

seeing in church. They may have dirty or inappropriate clothes. Give them grace. They may be hungry and eat every single fishy cracker in your nursery. Give them grace. They most likely will not have a diaper bag or a change of clothes. Give them grace. They might smell like stale alcohol, cigarette smoke, or pot. Give them grace. They might act odd or say awkward things. Give them grace. They may not attend consistently, so they won't know the memory verse. Give them grace. They won't tithe. Give them grace. They may drive you completely nuts. Give them grace. They may rip down pictures on the wall or steal toilet paper to take home. Give them grace. No matter what they do or say, the attitude of your heart needs to be one of grace. The temptation is to expect them to act the way you "should" act in church. But realizing they do not know how to act in church will open your heart in such a way that you can offer them the kind of grace that leads straight to Jesus.

> *Instead, be kind to each other, tenderhearted, forgiving one another, just as God through Christ has forgiven you.* Ephesians 4:32 (NLT)

The beginning phase of this type of ministry will stretch your church. It will stretch you. It certainly stretched me.

Something to Think About:

Is there a kid like Cameron in your ministry, even now, who comes to mind? If you were being totally honest, is there one kid who you would feel a little relieved not to have in class again next week? Is there one kid you try to avoid, who drains so much out of you that you feel very strong emotions every time you think of him or her? If so, I want you to think of that one. The hard one. The one you can't figure out. The one who wants ALL of your attention, ALL of the time. I want you to pray for that kid. Right now. Go on, I'll wait.

Now, I want to encourage you to think of three tangible things you can do to reach out to the child God just laid on your heart. Can

GO

you go to a game or a concert? Can you help him with a school project? Can you stop over at her house with some supplies to make duct tape wallets or some other craft? Can you take him a book about something he is interested in? Once you have come up with a couple of ideas, I want you to pick one and do it. Don't just think about it. Make a plan, carve out the time, and then just go.

6. SUCCESS OR SIGNIFICANCE

How do you measure success in ministry? How do you judge effectiveness? Is it the number of salvations in one season? Is it the increase in attendance? Perhaps it is the amount of money in the bank account? I was thinking about all of these variables one year as we finished the season. I began trying to evaluate the program, but I kept finding myself up against a wall. How could I measure the success of our program? None of it really had anything to do with me. It was all about God and what He was choosing to do in each of our neighborhoods, yet I still had the sense that I wanted to examine our time with kids in order to improve and build upon it for the next year.

As I reflected on all of the transformation we were seeing in families, I realized that there was eternal significance in what we were doing. The Lord revealed an important aspect about the ministry to me—it isn't about success; it is about significance. Anything that I could call a success was merely temporary. Yes, our attendance was higher than it had been the previous year, but soon, once the weather got bad, that might change. Yes, we had built up the reputation of the program as one that sincerely sought to help our community, but the true tests of whether or not what we were doing had any real impact couldn't be measured. It was about empty hearts being filled and broken lives getting pieced back together. It was about the changes in entire families and neighborhoods as the paths people were on changed. Those were the things that God cared about.

GO

When I realized that, I was able to let go of trying to measure our success. Instead, I began to focus on measuring significance. As my evaluations turned into goals for the next year, I now placed a standard on every aspect of our program. Was our ministry going to lead to a measure of significance? Would it propel us forward in such a way that the kingdom of God would be changed? As I held our program up to this standard, a word from Christian speaker and author Margaret Feinberg caught my heart. She mentioned the fact that every moment of our lives carries eternal significance.[2] Was I living as if that were true? Are you? How would we live differently if we really believed that statement? How would it change the way we speak to people, the way we organize our thought life, and the way we hold on to things that we should forgive?

As I realized the full weight of that statement, I re-evaluated the way we were running our program. We only had about an hour at each site, maybe less if the kids didn't stay the entire time. A question I thought through may be helpful to ask yourself as well, as you evaluate your own programs.

How was I using the moments God had given me?

Was I executing a thought-out plan, or was I simply winging it? Many people, myself included, have made the statement that they are going to depend on the Holy Spirit to lead them where they need to go. I agree that we need to leave room in our messages for the Holy Spirit to work. If the Holy Spirit, however, can work through our spontaneous and possibly distracted minds, how much more effective could the Holy Spirit be if we carved out time beforehand to make a plan? Having a plan and teaching with intention and purpose does not prevent the Holy Spirit from guiding and leading you. He can make a spiritual impact *through* your plan. You can follow His leading as

---

2 Feinberg, Margaret. (margaretfeinberg.com), author of *Fight Back with Joy* and *Flourish*.

you sense His presence while you are teaching. What I have found oftentimes is that God takes something I have planned, and He adds Himself to it. Those moments do not have to be long in order to be effective. The Holy Spirit can do more for a kid in 30 seconds than we can in an entire year of curriculum. Allow for that, but also allow for the realization that there *will* be distractions. There will be things that just don't work. There will be times where you think things will go one way and they quickly spiral out of control. If you have a plan going into your lesson, you are much more likely to be effective as you minister despite the challenges.

That being said, I have seen people go into a ministry opportunity with 16 pages of notes that they plan to read aloud. Although that may be appropriate or effective in some scenarios, I have yet to see that as a good way to deal with kids on the street. You need to be prepared, but the lesson needs to be *in* you more than *in front of* you. In the resource section of this book (pg. 129), I have included a sample semester of curriculum based on what I have done in the past. You will see that everything we do or say is kept to one page for easy reference as you are teaching the kids. We use the same format each week, and then change the topic as we go along. I ask each of my teams to use their own personal stories and struggles as they teach the kids. You know your own story better than anyone, and when you share what is already inside you, you will come across as authentic. That authenticity is what kids are looking for. They don't necessarily want someone who is perfect. They want someone they can connect with who is real.

Was I being intentional with the way we ran our games? Games are often the favorite part of the Sidewalk session for the kids. They are what we use to draw them in, but up until now, our games had been disconnected from the rest of the program. They were fun, engaging, and served a purpose, but if I want to work within the framework of

GO

"every second" counting, could I do better? Instead of just being fun, was there a way to integrate the game into a portion of the lesson so it could lead to a teachable moment?

Was our worship time effective? Was I really teaching the kids what it meant to worship, or was I simply playing music and asking the kids to sing along? What about transitions? Were we wasting time getting from one segment of the lesson to another? Those transition times seemed to be when we lost some of the kids. I started to think through every part of our program, making sure I was making the best use of our time. Every moment counts. This became my new mission—to make sure we were using wisely every precious second God gave us with His kids.

• • •

I remember one Sunday morning when I was going through this transition in thinking. I was teaching in the kids' class, and we had been talking to them about giving. I had shared with them some of the needs we saw when we traveled on missions' trips overseas. We had another trip coming up, so the kids were helping to decide what need to fund. After praying about it, they decided on giving toward food for the kids we would be serving in a garbage dump in Kenya. There was a village we worked with that literally lived inside a garbage dump. Orphans, widows, and entire families lived there because it was the only place where they could find even a small scrap of food. I thought that teaching kids, especially ones with very little money, about tithing and giving would be difficult. But in reality, the opposite was true. Kids naturally have a tendency to be moved to give toward a need they care about, especially if it involves other kids. Kids from homes that don't have a lot understand the need on a different level. They understand the hunger pangs that come on the third day in a row without food. They understand what it's like to be cold because your shoes have holes in them, and you own only one sock. They understand not being able to do homework because you don't have any pencils or the electricity has been shut off and you can't see anything. They understand what going without feels like.

I didn't realize how much my story about the kids in Kenya had touched my class until the end of the morning, when we asked the kids to give toward the offering. We had been talking about our giving challenge for a couple of weeks, but I was blown away by how generous the kids were. We had been working on this series for a while so they could get an idea of how finances work in the Kingdom of God. It was awesome to see God's kids giving to a need for kids they had never met. One young six-year-old girl brought all of her tooth fairy money from the first tooth she had ever lost. Another brought her birthday money. One boy had been doing extra chores and helping neighbors in order to save some money to give. Then came Cade. Cade was from a family that were regulars at our food pantry. There were a lot of kids in Cade's house, and various people were always in and out of their home. As Cade walked up to place his offering in the bucket, he very intentionally laid in $5.

"Are you sure, Cade?" I asked him.

"I'm sure, Ms. Rachael. That money is for the kids." He reassured me that he knew what he was doing.

I didn't doubt Cade's sincerity. He was one of the most sincere kids we had. I just knew how much $5 meant to a kid like Cade. Touched, I prayed for God to bless Cade as I watched him walk back to his seat.

It wasn't until the next day that I realized the full cost of Cade's offering. About 9 o'clock in the morning, my phone rang. The angry man on the other end was accusing me of stealing money from his son who had come to church the day before. Once I was able to get him to calm down, I learned some more details. It was Cade's dad. He knew Cade had earned $5 for mowing the neighbor's lawn a couple of days before. When he asked Cade about the money, Cade shared with

GO

his dad that he had given it as an offering at church. Angered, his dad called me, wanting to get the $5 back.

"Sir," I began, "I asked Cade if he was sure, and he told me that it was his money, and that he knew what he was doing. I can assure you that I did not steal anything, rather Cade gave to a need that he felt strongly about."

"Well, what did you do with all the money?" he asked.

"I gave it to the church treasurer, and it was put with the money we sent to Africa." I went on to explain exactly what we were doing with the funds, and his tone softened a bit. As I was starting to explain to him how proud I was of Cade, he hung up on me.

Later that afternoon, I went to visit Cade, just to make sure he was okay. As I pulled into his neighborhood, I found him riding his bike around the parking lot.

"Is everything okay?" I asked.

"Yeah," he replied, with his head down.

"Cade, can you tell me why your dad was so upset?" I asked.

"$5 is how much a hit costs," he replied, but I still didn't understand. "Of heroin," he explained.

He lifted his head to look at me, and at that moment I noticed the black eye. This was an 8-year-old little boy! I reached out to him, shocked at the realization of what had transpired that day. I had no idea that scenarios like this existed in our town. Of course, you hear about problems like this on the news, but realizing it is happening to kids and it's a regular part of their lives is sickening.

"I knew this would happen, Ms. Rachael. It's okay," he tried to comfort me. The fact that this behavior was part of his reality made me want to throw up.

"This is not okay, Cade. This is not okay. I'm so sorry this has happened to you," I stammered a little over my words. Even though protective services were already at work in the home, it was not enough to heal their family. (Cade has since been placed in a different home in a different town.)

As I prayed for Cade that evening and the impact of the full cost of the offering Cade gave, I realized he had given more freely—more sacrificially—than many adults I know. He knew what the punishment would be for giving that money. *He knew*, yet he gave anyway. Why? I believe it was the movement of God on his heart. Never did I think for one second that Sunday morning that there would be such a cost, even a consequence, for his gift. But he did. I wondered about my own kids, and even myself. I wondered if I would have given that money, knowing what was waiting for me on the other side of my obedience to God's voice. There was *significance* to what Cade did that day, making the decision to give.

It breaks my heart that a scenario like this one is even possible, yet it is the harsh reality for many of our kids. Sometimes, even doing what is right and following through on what we are teaching them is contrary to what they have been taught in the home. We are battling generations of a certain way of thinking. Yet somehow, as we spent a few weeks teaching the kids about giving sacrificially, Cade heard our words, and they took root in his heart. In moments like these, I realize there is a measure of effectiveness in what we are doing. There is significance to the fact that Cade stood up for what God was placing on his heart—no matter what the cost. I pray that I will have such obedience.

Something to Think About:

As you embark on adding an outreach ministry to your already busy life and schedule, I want to encourage you in an area that I struggled with initially. I was already running an infant, preschool, and elementary program, as well as writing curriculum and teaching Wednesday nights. As a mom of three young children, my plate was

GO

already full. In order to do all the things that needed to get done in a week, I started to make a list. As I headed into my office, I had an agenda and a plan. My ordered plan needed to succeed if I was going to accomplish what I needed to for that week. As I made myself a cup of coffee, I started to review my list. As I was reading through it, the phone rang. One of our kids had been taken by child protective services, and one of our volunteers was calling to let me know. Even though we saw this coming—had even spoken with a caseworker—the reasons the kids was taken were sickening. I took a few moments to encourage our volunteer, and we made a plan to follow up with the kids in that neighborhood who were sure to have questions. After we prayed together, I hung up the phone, only to find an unexpected visitor standing at my door. She was having an issue with her daughter stealing at school and wondered if I had any parenting tips for her. We spent some time looking at biblical ways to handle the situation, and I went through a parenting plan with consequences for her to implement in the home. After she left, I was called into the lead pastor's office for a meeting about an outreach for a foster and adoption ministry that we were part of. After the meeting, I had to pick up my daughter from kindergarten. When we got back, I had a financial form to fill out in order to get some much-needed funds for Christmas gifts for kids. After that was done, the phone rang again with a request from someone wanting to know how they could get involved with our outreach program. Before I knew it, the end of the day had come, and not one thing was crossed off my list. Actually, the entire week was like that. Each day was consumed with things that seemed to take me away from the work I knew I was supposed to be doing.

Toward the end of the week, I found myself complaining to God on my drive to the church. As I was listing the things I had planned

GO

to do that week, my tirade about my agenda was interrupted by that still, small voice that is able to calm my spirit with a simple question.

"What about MY agenda?" God asked me.

Immediately, I felt convicted about the mini temper tantrum I was having. Yes, I had a list of seemingly important things to do, but God prompted me, "What if the interruptions WERE the important things?"

As I thought back to what was actually taking my time that week—what the interruptions were—I realized that they were all ministry opportunities to reach kids and families God had placed in my path. God had given me the ability to be a voice that could speak into several situations. Wasn't that, in reality, what I had been called to do? Was my to-do list really that important?

This was a turning point for me in ministry. I still make to-do lists, and I still obviously have an agenda of what I would like to get done in a week. But every day, as I start on my way to the office, I pray for God's agenda to take the place of my agenda. This does take some discernment because not every interruption will be from God. But taking on an attitude that makes room for God to move in our daily lives will allow us to have the precise moments for which He has placed us in our positions—moments of significance.

Some moments do not feel like successes. That's part of ministry. But there will also be moments, as you push through, that will show you how much God is growing the kids you work with. The fear of failure can sometimes hold us back from what God wants to do. Is God preparing you for a ministry of significance? I believe He is. If you allow Him, He will enable you to reach into places that otherwise are closed. He will give you a unique vision to make a significant change in an otherwise unreached place. Take a breath, make a plan, and pray for His agenda instead of your agenda. Then just go.

7. WORDS

"Give me vision, Lord." That's my prayer every year. Before curriculum, before volunteers, before even praying for the sites, my prayer is always for the Lord to give me a fresh vision. Each year, as God lays something on my heart, it does not replace the vision of the previous year—it builds upon it.

Last year, as I was praying about the start of our Sidewalk season, God led me to a passage of Scripture that has become almost the platform upon which we build our outreach ministry. I was studying in the NASB, and I came upon a verse I had read many times before in other translations. This time the verse jumped off the page to me.

Therefore, thus says the LORD, *"If you return, then I will restore you—Before Me you will stand;* **And if you extract the precious from the worthless, You will become My spokesman.** Jeremiah 15:19 (NASB), emphasis added

Extract the precious. Those words just spoke something into my heart. Isn't that what God was doing with me? He didn't see all the brokenness of my past. He saw something precious in me, and little by little, He was extracting it in such a way that it was becoming something of value. I could see His fingerprints all over the page as I realized God's Word truly is living and active. Backing up a bit, I realized the process of returning to Him day by day as I read His Word was the very thing that was restoring me. Instead of allowing me

GO

to be broken and crippled by the pain of my past, He was picking me up and sustaining me as I stood before Him. Now, through that process, He was giving me a voice. I had opportunities to speak to these children He had placed in my life.

I shared this message with our Sidewalk teams and explained how the concept of extracting the precious would be the theme verse for our year. I asked them to pray for God to give them wisdom as they went into each of our neighborhoods. I placed the verse above my desk, so I could keep it fresh in my mind and heart as I wrote curriculum and prepared for our season.

By the time our Sidewalk program started later that summer, I was busy, knee-deep in the needs of the kids we were meeting and loving. One particular week, I was really excited about a lesson we were teaching. My family had recently purchased a cow for our freezer and received some various weird cuts of meat that came along with that. One of them was the tongue. Every time I got a package of hamburger out of my freezer, there sat that tongue, almost taunting me. Until one day, I decided to use it at Sidewalk. As I defrosted it on my kitchen counter, I watched as my children and husband walked nervously past it in the kitchen. After I reassured them that it wasn't dinner, I explained my plans to them. I wanted to teach the children about the power of our words. My plan was to have a Styrofoam cooler covered with a black cloth and explain to the kids that I had something very powerful inside of the box. I was going to tell them I had the most powerful weapon in the world inside the box. I would even offer a prize if they could guess correctly what I had.

As I taught this object lesson at the first of our sites, none of the children—or even the adults—guessed there was a tongue in my box. When I did the big reveal, their reactions were priceless. Some were intrigued, and some were disgusted. Most of them had never seen a cow tongue before, so this was something that completely held their

GO

attention. It gave me the opportunity to share with them that there is so much power in our words. We talked about how our words have the ability to heal or destroy. As the kids were starting to understand, I felt led to ask them if there were words spoken in their lives that made an impact on them. A couple of kids shared some words someone had used to encourage them. Then it came time for young Jemma's turn. As she raised her hand, the spaghetti strap of her too-big tank top slipped down her shoulder, and she held it up with the other hand. Jemma and I actually had just met that day. Her sisters had come to Sidewalk before, and I had seen her playing in the neighborhood, but I had never had an opportunity to have a conversation with her. She was very thin, maybe about 8 years old, and she dressed in clothes that looked like they belonged to a much older teen.

"Jemma," I called on her. "Why don't you share with us the words that made an impact on you?" I asked.

She looked me straight in the eyes and responded, "My dad says I'm worthless."

Wow. Sucker punch to the stomach. I made eye contact with one of our volunteers, and I found myself quickly praying about how to respond. In the midst of my inability to form a response, God directed me in the words to say.

"Extract the precious from the worthless," He reminded me.

The exact words Jemma had said were the ones that God had prepared me for earlier that year. I felt Him speak right to my heart: "This moment. This moment right now is the one that I have been preparing you for this whole summer."

Pushing my emotions aside, I immediately felt the presence of God as I spoke life over this little girl. Taking her hands in mine, bringing my face close to hers, I responded in a moment of compassion that I am sure was fueled by the heart of God Himself.

GO

"Jemma, you are not worthless. God says that you are precious and worth dying for. He loves you so much, and you are a treasure to Him."

As I spoke, I could see tears forming in her eyes. All the other kids, lost in the moment, were so silent we could hear the sprinklers kick on in the grassy field across the parking lot. Her heart was open, and that was the moment she prayed with me to receive Jesus. The impact of that moment is not lost on me. I will never forget it because it was a turning point in ministry for me.

I thought I had come up with a great way to teach the kids about something relevant. Little did I realize that the Lord was setting up an opportunity to speak to me as well. The words that we speak over these kids are not just about our lesson for the day or something fun that will keep their attention. The words we speak over the kids we serve have the power of life or death. Reaching into the heart of a child with a word from God is a very powerful thing. It not only changes them—it changes you.

As I packed up and left, I felt the Lord very clearly remind me again of that word in Jeremiah:

Extract the precious from the worthless and you will become my spokesman.

As I prayed for this little girl and her heart, God burned something deep into mine. "You are my spokesman. The words you speak to these kids are My words. Keep loving them, keep serving them, keep reaching them." As I realized the lesson God had been preparing me for, I couldn't help but realize that He had a plan and a purpose for every single one of these kids. Every. Single. One. He sees them cry, He hears their hearts, and He longs for someone to reach into that darkness and extinguish it with the light of the gospel.

Heading on to our next site for the day, I realized I would probably not have the same type of "God moment" that I had at the first site.

Nonetheless, this next site was filled with tween boys, and I knew they would love the gross cow tongue. Our team prepared, and we started out much the same way. This time, though, all the boys wanted to touch the tongue, and the situation was much less somber than it had been at the previous site. We asked the kids the same questions, and it came to be the turn of one of the older boys.

"Naveen, what are some words that have made an impact on you?" He pondered my question for a minute, and then looked down at the ground.

"Well," he started, "these words."

"These words?" I asked.

"Yes, these words. You come here, and you tell us all this stuff that we have never heard before. And it makes things better." He finished answering and then looked away.

I think he was a little concerned about what the other boys were going to think or say. But then, they all started chiming in about how the things we taught them were starting to change how they handled situations in their lives, how they felt about themselves, and how they understood who God was. I have never been so humbled as I was in that moment.

Sometimes we so easily take for granted the things we know to be true from our lives in the church and our education in God's Word. This opportunity gave me a fresh perspective on how it must feel to hear the truth for the first time.

Later that week, as I was leaving the neighborhood after a visitation, something at the corner of my eye caught my attention. I looked over at the falling-down trailer that was the home to some of our kids. Above the doorway, written in what I think was chalk, were the words, "Jesus is Lord." It was written in a child's handwriting, and I was pretty sure I knew which child. I stopped my car in disbelief and took in everything I was seeing. Seven children, and sometimes more, were living in that tiny trailer. There was rarely enough food to go around, and the kids were in obvious need of clothes and basic hygiene items. We worked hard at making sure they had the basics, but the environment the kids were living in was not ideal. As I looked at this doorway, I remembered the lesson we had taught just before Easter, talking about the significance of aligning yourself with God. They were listening. Now, months later, this was their public declaration to everyone who would drive by in that hard neighborhood. Jesus is Lord. They were hearing what we were teaching, and it was starting to sink down into their hearts.

• • •

"My name is Victor and I do not want a sandwich." The declaration came from a little boy who was a little unsure of himself and almost seemed afraid of the other kids. After taking a juice box, Victor sat down next to me as we were getting ready to start our lesson. Victor had not come to Sidewalk before, but he was very well behaved and listened intently. I do not remember exactly what our lesson was that day, but I do remember Victor coming to me afterwards. The rest of the kids were playing, and Victor took me by the hand.

"I have something to tell you," he said, as he led me over to the fence along the back of the playground. We sat down with our backs to the fence, and I waited quietly as he gathered himself. "I have really bad nightmares. Every night, I dream of the fire. And my grandma dying."

As I let him speak, I carefully observed some things I hadn't seen before. His legs were covered in scars—scars that made it obvious there had been some significant trials in his young life. As he laid his little head on my shoulder, I could sense he was in need of some comfort, so I pulled him into a hug. We sat there silently for a few minutes, and I struggled to come up with words. Initially, I didn't have any. The few sentences he shared spoke of such pain, both physical and emotional, that I didn't want to say anything to make it worse. But realizing he had come to me for help, I knew I had to share something. I stood up in front of these kids, telling them about a God who was bigger than anything. Did I believe He was bigger than nightmares? And fires? And death? I did. Victor needed to know those things about God too. We sat for almost an hour, talking about different stories from the Bible and my own life. My prayer for Victor that day was for peace. I explained to him what peace was and how it worked. He was so desperate for peace that he teared up when I explained to him how God talks about how His perfect peace can guard our heart and mind. As we parted ways that day, I held Victor's prayer close to my heart. I asked God to intervene in such a way that Victor would be able to sense it, immediately, that night.

So many kids that we have met over the last couple of years have needs far beyond what we could even imagine in a small community like ours. In some circumstances we have become almost surrogate parents for a lot of kids, just by consistently speaking life over and into them on a regular basis. A girl that used to bang her head against the wall for attention doesn't anymore because she realizes she is beautiful, inside and out. A child from a rough home knows that God keeps His promises, and so does Ms. Rachael. A young boy considers my husband his best friend because he's the only man in his life who is nice to him. The list goes on and on. The value that is placed on words by kids who need them is immeasurable. The kinds of words we often take for granted are outright life-changing for some of the kids we meet.

Something to Think About:

I want you to do something with me for a minute. I want you to think back to the toughest, hardest, most hurtful words anyone ever spoke to you. I bet you don't have to think too long, do you? For most

GO

of us, even the thought of those words can bring back some pretty powerful emotions. How did you heal from those words? For me, it took someone coming into my life and not only refuting those words, but replacing them with something else. Now, I would like you to think back to the most powerful words anyone has ever spoken over you—something that someone said at some point in your life that took root in you. For me, they were words written on a card I received in the mail from one of my youth leaders. I can almost guarantee that if I asked her about it today, she probably would not even remember what she said. But I do. Think about the contrast in emotions between the two scenarios that we just thought about. Do you see what I am talking about? Great power dwells in your words. As you step into the calling God has for you, I believe He is going to use you to make an impact on the hearts of the kids in your community. Don't take that lightly. It's a very powerful thing to be able to speak into someone's life. As you consider the impact words can have, my challenge to you is to allow yourself to be placed in situations where you have the chance to speak into the life of a child. Perhaps it is through a formal lesson or perhaps it is through a conversation that happens naturally through relationship. Either way, kids in your community need to hear the words that the gospel teaches us. They need to hear about the hope found only in Jesus, and they need you to be the one to bridge that gap. Go find them, and tell them. Just go.

8. FEAR OR FIGHT

"You got a voicemail about Sidewalk."

It was Wednesday morning, and our Sidewalk outreach program was scheduled for later that evening. Word was spreading about how much families in the community liked our program. We were starting to get calls from people who had found our flyers and wanted more information. As I balanced a basket full of supplies on one hip, I half-heartedly listened to the voicemail while I found a pen in the drawer to take down the phone number. As I flipped over a piece of paper to scribble on, my stomach started to ache as I heard the words on the other end of the phone.

"This is Kelly, the manager from Gill. You can no longer come down here to do your program. Thanks."

What? Who was Kelly? And why? What had we done wrong? As I hurriedly scrolled through the caller ID to retrieve her number, my mind started racing. Had we done something? Maybe they needed us to switch to a different day? Maybe they wanted us to switch to a playground instead of the community center. So many thoughts went through my mind as I left my own, cheerful message on the answering machine of the Gill Commons manager. I tried not to sound too desperate as I pleaded with the machine for her to call me back. As I wandered to my office, I tried to keep occupied, sorting the prizes I had ordered from Oriental Trading and praying silently. Thinking about the kids in the neighborhood, I was overcome with the feeling

GO

of disappointing them, and I quietly wept. Waiting for a call back became almost painful as I tried to focus on the work in front of me. Trying in my mind to prepare the questions I would ask, I gathered myself and wrote them down.

About lunchtime, I received a phone call from Kelly. She briefly and abruptly explained to me that because the housing project was government property, we were not allowed to do any religious programming there. I was pretty sure she was wrong, but not really knowing the law, I didn't know how to respond. I asked her why we had been allowed for the entire past year to have a program in the community, and all of a sudden we were being stopped. She had no answer. I asked her who made this decision, and she told me that the government did. I thanked her for her time and hung up the phone. Surely this wasn't right. I mean, I had watched on television as people prayed on the White House lawn in the past. I knew different churches hosted Vacation Bible Schools in various areas of the community—some of which were at government-owned playgrounds and parks. I knew we had to fight this, or at least question it, but I had no idea where to start.

As you get started in your own outreach ministry, you potentially may come up against someone trying to put a stop to what you are doing. Especially in the beginning, you may be met with resistance, and it is helpful to know ahead of time what the laws are in your state. Also, as Christians, we have certain federal rights that you should research before you get started. That way, when and if you are questioned, you will know exactly how to respond. We are called to live as people of peace, but I also believe we have a very real enemy who will fight us any way he can in order to maintain control of the lives of kids who are lost and hurting. As Christians, the time has come for us to fight back. Many of our ministry sites are on private property. As long as you have permission from the owner of the property, you

GO

are protected; however, if you are on publicly owned property or government property, you will want to research exactly how you are protected by law.

As I sat at my desk praying for direction, I had no idea where to start. But I did know two very important things: I knew God had called us to start this ministry, and I also knew God had a plan for our kids. So as I prayed for wisdom, I asked God to intervene. I started to research the Housing Authority in our town, and I learned that the area we had been in was actually one of several operated by the same governing board. I was able to track down the head of the board, and I called him. Leaving a voicemail, I explained who I was and tried to portray how imperative it was that he call me back. Calling again later that day, I was told by his secretary that he would not be in for the next couple of days. Clearly, we were going to have to cancel our Sidewalk session in the neighborhood that evening.

Heartbroken, I went down to the neighborhood to see the kids at the time we normally do Sidewalk. Already, a bunch of kids were there waiting for us, ready to help set up. When I explained to them that we would not be able to have Sidewalk, they were very upset. Some cried, some got angry, some immediately ran over to the housing manager's office and wrote notes that they slipped under her door. As I watched the reaction of my little friends, I realized there was no way I could let this go. We had to fight this. After I spent some time with the kids, I walked back to my van. When I got there, three girls were waiting for me, begging me to do whatever it took to get Sidewalk back into the neighborhood. I promised them that I would do whatever I could. As I got into my van to leave, I caught something out of the corner of my eye. "Please don't leave" was written in the dust on the back window. Tears ran down my face that evening as I drove away. I resolved right then and there that if there was a way to get back, I would. Instead of doing Sidewalk that night, our team gathered to pray. Even though

GO

we didn't know the way forward, God did, and we were going to need His help to figure this out.

I spent the next couple of days researching the laws in our area. From what I could find, nothing was legally preventing us from providing a Christian-based program on government property. I finally got a phone call back from the Housing Authority supervisor, and I started with my questions. He repeated that they had a policy preventing anyone from offering any type of "religious programming" on government-owned property. He asked why we were even going there and who asked us to go. I explained that we went because we saw a need. I talked about how our program was not just about the formal lesson we did, but also about serving the community in general. I explained how we did a mobile food pantry, had a mentorship program, helped with school and tutoring, and met some of the basic needs the kids had. Although he agreed that all of these things were necessary, he objected to the fact that our program was gospel centered. He explained that if he were to allow us to present the gospel, he would also have to allow the KKK and perhaps snake handlers to come into the area to lead a children's program as well. I had to keep myself from laughing at him, and politely explained how our program was different from the types of groups he mentioned. By the end of the conversation, he had asked me to submit to him, in writing, everything we had been doing in the neighborhood with all the details of what our program encompassed. Immediately following our conversation, I emailed him a list of everything we had just talked about. It seemed as though he had softened a bit, and I was hopeful that he would allow us to continue, given everything we were doing to help the kids in the community.

After I received his reply, however, my hopes were deflated. Although he recognized that our attempts to help were addressing valid needs, and even went so far as to say he was grateful for some of the ways we were helping, he could not allow us to continue as we had been. He would allow us to offer programming—would even allow us to use the microphone and play music—but we could not mention God, Jesus, the Bible, church, or pray. We could teach "moral" lessons but could not include our reason for teaching them. We could hand out our flyers announcing the weekly events, but we would have to take the words "Sunday school" off of them. Basically, we could do everything we had been doing as long as we did not give any public indication that we were compelled to do so by our faith.

Even though I realized these mandates were stifling our rights, I agreed, for the time being, in order to get back into the neighborhood. It would be challenging, and we would fight it, but at least we would be back with the kids who needed us. I thanked him as politely as I could and called our lawyer as soon as I got off the phone. Our local attorney really had never been up against anything like this before, so we needed to find the help of someone who had, and quickly.

The search for help led us to the organization, Alliance Defending Freedom, or ADF. ADF describes itself as a "non-profit legal organization building an alliance to keep the door open for the Gospel by transforming the legal system and advocating for religious liberty, the sanctity of life, and marriage and family."[3] When we reached out to them, they responded almost immediately. Within two weeks, ADF sent a team member to Meadville from Arizona. After speaking with their legal counsel, we realized we were the victims of viewpoint discrimination, which we were protected from under our First Amendment rights. ADF agreed to help us, and they laid out a plan to try to get us back into the neighborhood.

I had previously sent letters to state officials but had been told that the matter lay within the jurisdiction of the Housing Authority officials. ADF picked up where we left off. After a two-month-long

---

3 World Christian Resources Directory. Christian Legal Resources. (www.missionresources.com)

GO

process, the work of ADF paid off. They won the right for us to get back into the neighborhood without having to go to court. Their knowledge of the law and their willingness to fight for us were enough to prompt the Housing Authority to seek their own legal counsel. As a result, they had to change their ruling. We have since been allowed to go back with a full program and offer every aspect of the ministry we had originally started.

While celebrating the lifting of the restrictions, we were excited to be able to fully plan a gospel-centered program for the following summer. What we did not anticipate happening was the publicity that resulted from our fight. ADF shared our story on their website and social media, and other Christian media sources also covered the story. Consequently, other neighborhoods in our community heard about our program, and doors were opened for us to expand the program citywide. In addition, this case helped establish protocol for other churches or outreach ministries that might face opposition. They could now reference our case and hopefully avoid the discrimination that we struggled against. We realized God had a plan to work through the mess, and the result would make an impact not just on our city but on other cities with similar challenges.

> *You intended to harm me, but God intended it all for good. He brought me to this position so I could save the lives of many people.* Genesis 50:20 (NLT)

God's plan is never a backup plan or a plan B—it's the best plan.

Here is a link to one of the many news articles covering this story: http://christiannews.net/2015/05/03/church-regains-right-to-serve-housing-project-after-initially-booted-for-being-religious/

GO

My hope is that if you are up against a struggle, you can fight with some tools that have already been given to you through our experience. A legal battle is nothing compared to the fight we have in front of us as God leads us to kids who need us to be their champions.

Someone Has to Show Up

When we walked in the door, I was at a loss for words. I felt awkward as I paid my $7 to enter the room. While I took in all the unfamiliar faces and tried to swallow any fear or anxiety I had, I suddenly was pushed back by a small boy who had jumped to wrap his arms around me. As I looked down, I saw him—the reason we came. At six years old, little Ty had quickly become one of my favorites. I know we aren't supposed to have favorites, but he and I had been through thick and thin. After four years of loving him and investing in him, it was impossible not to feel attached to those big brown eyes and super cute braids.

As he looked up at me, excitedly showing me his balloon, the event felt more like a birthday party than a funeral dinner. I was quickly met by another small boy, Ty's cousin Josephus, who also held a special place in my heart. As they started to dance on the dance floor with their matching red shoes, I felt like crying. I'm not sure they even understood what was going on. We found a seat near the edge of the room and just watched them dancing, having a good time. I started to see a few familiar faces trickle into the room. Little Ty, the life of the party, seemed to enjoy keeping everyone happy as his dancing to the loud music entertained them.

I was distracted for a few minutes by a conversation with our bus director, who had come here with me, one town over into the darkest section of the area. Two white girls in that neighborhood after dark was probably not the safest thing, but our call to love those boys was greater than any reservations we might have had. When I looked up,

GO

I saw the brokenness. Heads bowed, tears running down cheeks, and loud sobs coming from somewhere deep inside. Addiction had taken a close family member through overdose, and this party was a benefit dinner to raise funds the day before the funeral. Drug overdose was common to this family, the struggle a constant presence in the lives of these kids.

Ty returned and I pulled my chair close and laid my hand on his back. He looked at me through teary eyes and said, "I'm never going to see her again."

"I know," I said.

As he put his head down, I could feel a mix of anger, fear, and sorrow just pouring out of his little body. I asked him if he wanted a hug. He shook his head no. I asked him if he wanted a tissue. He shook his head no. I asked if he wanted me to leave him alone. He shook his head no. So we sat. For a long time, we just sat. He cried; I prayed. In that moment, I had no words to comfort him. I had no prizes, candy, games, or object lessons that would help his little heart, but I did have my presence, my love, my consistency, and my compassion. Those are the things that speak in a place that is so dark light can hardly get in—the things you don't plan, but build over time. Because of our relationship—built upon countless sandwiches, afternoon visits, and encouraging words—I had earned the right to sit next to him. On the other side of the table sat my volunteer, who was doing a very similar thing with Josephus. She had spent countless hours with both of these boys and, as a result, had also gained a place to speak life over him despite the spirit of death that hung so closely over his head. As I exchanged a teary-eyed glance with her, we both could feel the heaviness these little boys were carrying.

I wish I could say there was a moment where some insightful, healing comment came to my mind, but really, all we did was sit in a dark, loud room with two hurting little boys. In moments like those,

GO

I don't even pretend to know what to do, but I still go. It is sometimes awkward, hard, uncomfortable, and inconvenient. Yet, somehow, God still uses those moments for His glory. He can speak promise into a child through our commitment to showing up. And in those dark moments, He can bring back words we have said to remind those kids that they are loved.

About an hour after we got there, Jaiden, a young boy I have come to love, walked through the door. Our eyes met, and he quickly came over for a hug. He was wearing one of the shirts I had dropped off for him earlier in the week. As he sat down, he started to explain his family relationship to almost everyone in the room. He asked us how we found the club we were in, and he was so surprised we had shown up for him. He asked us to stay all night, but as the night wore on, we recognized the fact that we would only be welcome in that environment for so long. We soon left with promises to see all of the boys over the weekend. After hugs and tears, we silently walked back to the car through the dark parking lot. While we drove home, my heart was so heavy. These little boys were like so many others in our community. They had become victims of the burden that overdoses, addiction, and substance abuse bring. They lived a life so different than my own children did. Their reality was so hard for me to stomach that I had a hard time sleeping that night.

But this is why...this is why we do what we do. This is why we don't stay within the four walls of our church. This is why we take the gospel INTO the neighborhoods. Someone has to go and share with these kids the hope that the gospel brings. Someone has to take the light into the darkness instead of running away from it. Someone has to show up.

GO

Something to Think About:

We were not given access to the hardest part of these kids' lives because we knocked on some doors one day in an outreach attempt. We were given access because we were consistent. We had proven we would show up when we said we would—even if it was raining, or cold, or inconvenient, or something else came up. Through that door of consistency, you walk through the yucky parts of kids' lives in order to teach them that something better is awaiting them.

Before I started this ministry, I simply did not have the capacity to imagine what some of these kids were going through—not in America, not in my community. We are just a small town with normal problems. Many of the neighborhoods we work in are not in prominent areas, but are tucked away and forgotten. One of our pastors who came from another state had lived in Meadville for almost four years with no idea that we even had low-income housing in our area. Out of sight, out of mind. For many churches, the focus is on the people who come. I believe that Jesus is now calling us to find the people who *don't* come. If you think you live in an area that does not have poverty, I would encourage you to do some digging. If God has led you to pick up this book, there is a reason. Maybe it is to go to the next town over. I know of some outreach ministries in larger cities that drive almost two hours, one-way, to reach the kids they minister to. I am positive there are kids closer to you than that.

The kids we have met in the short number of years we have been doing Sidewalk have so much against them. Many of them live in a constant state of fear. The abuse and misuse of a child's innocence is something that not only angers me but I am confident it angers God. Why aren't churches reaching these kids? It's time for the neglect to stop. It's time for someone to rise up to the call God is giving and just go.

9. HUNGRY

"I don't want chili for dinner."

My oldest daughter was with me, and she was complaining about what I had chosen to make for dinner. Truth be told, chili was not my favorite either, but it was cheap to make and easy to put in the slow cooker on a busy day. As she was complaining, mostly about the beans, I turned onto a road that was not our typical route home.

"Where are we going?" she asked. I had veered from our normal path, and she was becoming curious. As I turned down another side road, our destination became apparent. We were stopping at one of our outreach sites. It was not one of our designated outreach days, and I had not told her we were planning on going there after school. We had no team or truck. There were just the three of us—me, my daughter, and the Holy Spirit. Earlier in the day, I had been working on my to-do list, putting items in order of priority. Visiting a site was not on the list. This was already a full day, and the evening was going to be even more full because we had a life group followed by an evening service. As I was looking over my list, however, I felt the Holy Spirit nudging me to go down to one of our outreach sites to visit the kids. I started to compile my list of excuses—all the reasons I couldn't go and things that wouldn't get done because of the time it would take. This sense of calling cut through my emotion and attitude.

"Just go," the Holy Spirit said.

I often am asked how I know the Holy Spirit is speaking, how I

GO

know it's God's voice and not my own. It would really be great if I could tell you some glorious answer about doves and bells or something. But really, I know it's Him because I have been disobedient. A lot. So many times in my life I have heard that still, small voice, and because it is... well...still and small, it has been easy to ignore. Yet, the product of my disobedience has been hard-learned lessons about how God has tried to parent me, protect me, bless me, and teach me. If only I would have listened. So now, instead of ignoring, I started listening. One time when I was young, I was told that listening to God is like hearing radio static. You turn on the radio and hear some words through a lot of noise. You can either turn the knob in the direction of the correct station, or you can turn it away. Being obedient is kind of like turning the knob in the right direction. Eventually, things become clear. I also learned to stop allowing so much noise in my life.

As my daughter and I drew close to the site, I swallowed the lump that started to rise a little in my throat. I typically did not come to this neighborhood without my husband because it is notorious for being a little rough. I knew God was sending us here today, but I had no idea why. I pulled the car into my normal parking spot, and I silently prayed. Normally when I went there, I had a plan. I'm a planner. I've always been told that if you don't have a plan for the kids, they will have a plan for you. But today was different—I didn't have the security of notes, games, or a prepared Scripture. I had no reason to be down in that neighborhood. I had no expectation, no props, no prizes. But God...He had a plan. As my daughter and I walked over to one of the lots, I saw many of my little friends sitting by the side of the road. We headed toward them, my daughter, walking alongside me, still silently stewing about beans in her dinner. As I met the group, I recognized about ten kids, and a few more must have been siblings. As they realized who I was, the kids welcomed us with great excitement, and they all fought for time to tell me about their day at school. We were there about an hour, just laughing and talking with kids who needed someone to laugh and talk with them. As I was listening to stories about homework and teachers and gym class, I looked down to notice a blue and white box of pancake mix. The top was torn off, but I recognized it as one of the boxes we had given away in our mobile food pantry the week before. I wondered what it was doing there but easily dismissed it as I continued my conversation with three young girls about the cutest boys in second grade.

In the next few moments, my heart broke for these children I had now come to care so much about. I watched as the oldest, probably about 10 years old, picked up the box of pancake powder and dished it out into at least ten eager little hands. As they licked the powder out of their hands and put them out for a refill, I was initially disgusted and asked them what they were doing. Micky, one of the girls, explained that this was their dinner. They had enough to share, so they would all get dinner that night. Dinner. Dry, generic, pancake mix that they ate out of their hands. I felt my throat tighten as I fought back the tears, and made eye contact with my own daughter. Her eyes were so big as she watched these kids, and then they offered her some. She politely declined, and we realized this wasn't just about the pancake batter. This was about absent parents and hungry children. This was about food stamps and welfare checks not actually meeting the needs of the kids the way the government says they are supposed to. This was about the disconnect between the local church and the neighborhoods surrounding them. This was about me not realizing I could never reach empty hearts if I didn't reach empty bellies. This was about realizing that this broke God's heart more than it broke mine. As I took all this in, I knew we would have to start feeding our kids as much and as often as we could. Yes, they are supposed to have government services. Yes, they are supposed to have parents. Yes, children's protective services are supposed to prevent or stop things like this

GO

from happening. But they don't. All across America, they don't. Every night kids go to bed hungry—hungry for food, hungry for attention, hungry for love. As the church, meaning those who profess to love Jesus, we have to wake up and realize this issue is not unique to one community. This issue is replicated in every state and every city. Cities that have churches. And Christians.

I wish I could say that I knew exactly what to do at that point. I didn't. For a short-term solution, what I did was pray God would show me a way to help. I ran over to our emergency food pantry at the church and grabbed boxes of cereal. It was what we had, and I knew it would fill up some bellies for the night. After dropping the cereal and milk back off to the kids, hugging them all with promises of the fun games we would play later in the week, my daughter and I walked silently back to the car. I was so lost in my own shock and grief over the situation the kids were in I almost didn't see the single tear roll down my daughter's cheek. When we got back in the car, I watched her put her seat belt on. We sat in silence for a few minutes. I hadn't realized it was so bad. This was America—stuff like this wasn't supposed to happen here. But it does. And our churches are filled with people who don't know that it does. My daughter's words interrupted my thoughts.

"I will never complain about chili again," she whispered softly. Me either, dear one. Me either.

Hungry Bellies, Hungry Souls

Are there needs in your community that you aren't seeing? Ask God to give you an open mind and an obedient heart. I can guarantee you that He will start to show you what breaks His.

Two days later, I was ready. That was the same week the Housing Authority had told us we were no longer allowed to do Sidewalk Sunday school in the community. Because it was late September, many

GO

people had expressed the opinion that we should just close up shop for the season, fight the battle with Housing over the winter, and come back strong in the spring. I would be lying if I said I hadn't considered that option myself. Housing was putting so many limitations on us I wasn't sure we could even pull off a successful program for the kids. It was frustrating because we had worked so hard to build up a program that was working well. The team was trained and confident at this point in the season. The whole reason for going into this neighborhood was to share the gospel—something that we were no longer able to do. All circumstances pointed toward failure.

But there was something in me—especially after witnessing the pancake batter scenario—that just could not walk away yet. So with some guidance from our church leadership, we planned an evening where we would talk to the kids about our friend Mo, instead of Moses, and play songs like "Big Big House" that did not say the name of God or Jesus. I did get some criticism for that, but can I let you in on a little secret? I didn't care. I have thick skin and sometimes do the opposite of what people tell me to do just because I like a challenge. I once ate an entire Sam's Club sized jar of pickles in one sitting just because my brother said I couldn't…even though I hated pickles. (Side note: Pickles and I have now reconciled our differences and enjoy a nice lunch together every now and then.) I knew that by altering our program we were not completely fulfilling our initial purpose for reaching out to this community; however, at this point in the year, the kids expected us. They knew why we were there; we had taught them salvation and discipled them all summer long. By not going—especially without notice—we would drop the momentum we had been building. One of the reasons this type of ministry works is because of consistency—being there when you say you are going to be there—despite the weather, despite the challenges, despite the restrictions. Many of these kids have had so many broken promises in

GO

their lives they simply do not trust adults. Breaking their trust by not showing up just wasn't an option.

So, armed with a giant tub of peanut butter, jelly, apples, and juice boxes, we set up our stage and got to work doing the best we could with the restrictions we had. I knew the kids had already learned so much throughout the summer from us, but this was a true test. As we rolled in, kids were already there, waiting for us—a lot of kids, actually. I was so glad we decided to follow through. Sometimes, if we are going to minister the gospel effectively, we have to do whatever it takes. Sometimes the "whatever" might have to take the form of PB and J.

The kids responded so incredibly well to our first night serving food. Kids who typically were quiet and reserved came alive and smiled and laughed. We could see that even though we were following the call to meet the needs of the kids spiritually, we had been missing their physical needs. We knew then and there that feeding the kids would always be a part of our program. At the end of the evening, our team was playing with the kids as we started to pack up our truck. While I was cleaning up some of the leftover sandwiches, I noticed a man in a wheelchair watching me from across the street. I smiled and walked over to him, asking if he would like a sandwich. Initially, he refused, but as I explained that they were extra and would otherwise go to waste, he got excited and followed me over to where I had been working. As I gave him most of our leftovers, we started to chat. He encouraged me in what we were doing and told me that he listened most days from his house nearby. He appreciated how much we cared about the kids in the community and told me he could see a difference in how the kids acted when we weren't there. I used the opportunity to explain our motivation for coming.

During our chat that evening, my new friend explained how he wanted to get his life right with God. I took the next few moments to

GO

pray with him, and he committed his heart to the Lord. As he thanked me and rolled away, I thought through what had just happened. That moment—that moment the enemy had tried to steal—was the very moment we watched God move.

I was uplifted and encouraged, and shared that great story with my team as we cleaned up.

The following Monday, I realized the impact our Sidewalk Sunday school program had made that night. We got the news that our new friend, the man in the wheelchair, had passed away the night before from a massive heart attack. God, in His grace, had given him the opportunity to hear the gospel at Sidewalk before his passing. This man was not attending a church. He often was not even accepted in his own community. This man did not come to Sidewalk because he heard fabulous preaching or anointed worship. In fact, that evening he had heard none of that because we weren't allowed to worship or even mention the name of God or Jesus according to Housing restrictions. Yet, the Spirit of the Lord had drawn him still. He came because we were meeting a need. We cannot underestimate the power meeting needs—basic needs—can have as a door to someone's heart.

What if we had not gone? What if we had listened to those who told us not to go? What if we had stopped for the season because the obstacles we were facing were too much or too hard? I am so incredibly thankful for the role of the Holy Spirit in the life of a believer. Despite the noise of the world, the noise in my heart was louder.

One of the scriptures God has given me for this ministry comes from the book of Luke 1:78-79 (NLT):

Because of God's tender mercy, the morning light from heaven is about to break upon us, to give light to those who sit in darkness and in the shadow of death, and to guide us to the path of peace.

Can't you just see this verse unfold in the story I shared? God's

GO

tender mercy was shown as my friend was given the opportunity to be guided into a path of peace, as he sat in the shadow of death. God's mercy. You simply cannot deny that the fingerprints of God were on that entire situation, and I am so thankful.

Something to Think About:

Inevitably, you will meet challenges as you get into this ministry. My challenges will look much different than your challenges, I am sure. Depending on the size of your town or city, you may have more or less regulation than we do. Depending on the culture in your area, you may not be as well received as we have been. Depending on your church leadership, you may have to fight a little harder to get the support for this type of program. My encouragement to you is to plow through, despite all of those challenges.

My friend Michael Chanley, from CM Connect (www.cmconnect.org), uses the theme of the rhino in his ministry, and I think it fits so well with this concept. Rhinos only go forward. They don't go backward. I love that. I actually have a few T-shirts with rhinos on them that I wear to meetings with people who may challenge me. It's passive-aggressive, I know, but it helps keep me focused. The reality is, you have a very real enemy who is fighting to keep his hands on these kids. Your job is to keep pushing back, no matter what, and use the challenges as stepping-stones. And realize this, you are not fighting alone. You serve a God who is notorious for making a way when there seems to be no way. This ministry is typically not something that is being done in most areas because it's hard. The challenges and many of the situations you see can be heartbreaking. But if you allow Him, God will move in and through you, even when you don't realize it, as long as you are obedient. Once that happens, something rises up in you. Knowing that the Holy Spirit is the one organizing these moments and that He has a plan to move and work makes you eager

GO

to continue to listen to Him the next time. It builds your faith and makes it a little easier to hear Him. As you start this ministry, the first couple of years will be tough, but they will be worth it. Be a rhino, keep moving forward, and just go.

10. OBEDIENCE AND EXPECTATION

I don't know if you are like me, but sometimes I forget that what I am doing is not a job—it's a calling. It's easy to forget that on Mondays.

Because we do what we do, week in and week out, we easily get caught up in all the things we have to accomplish. If you are overseeing more than one ministry department, the list quickly adds up. Creating volunteer schedules, ordering the Christmas musical, checking on the kids who didn't show up last week. Prepping preschool crafts, reordering prizes, e-mailing parents. Picking up goldfish crackers, researching gluten-free play dough options. The list goes on and on. Our tasks can easily overcome our passion if we let them.

One Monday, after a particularly long and event-filled weekend, my attitude was less than stellar. I woke up thinking about the long day ahead of me and sighed. It wasn't that I was burned out. It wasn't that I didn't enjoy what I was doing. It wasn't even that I wasn't looking forward to what was on my list. But I started out my day just going through the motions. I wasn't looking to God for anything big. We had just had a great Sunday the day before, and the kids' response was positive. Today was probably going to be a let down. We were headed to smaller sites for our Sidewalk ministry that day, and attendance was pretty much guaranteed to be low. The county fair—the biggest food fair this side of the Mississippi, I might add—had

GO

started the day before. Families that typically have no money still seem to find money to go to the fair. Our kids would probably be gone, it was hot out, and most of our workers couldn't make it for some reason or another.

I headed to the church and prepped my Sidewalk truck. I counted the juice boxes, made sure we had emergency sandwich supplies, and was soon on my way. I reviewed our rosters for the day's sites and quickly said a prayer over the day. As I arrived at our first site and set up, I looked around and realized how sparse the kids were. Usually by this time of day, at least a dozen or so would be waiting for us. Today there were three.

I set up our tarps, balloons, and props for the day. Soon, I realized our regular kids had come, helpful and ready for the first game. After setting up, I was quickly surrounded by about 25 kids—double the number we typically had on most days. As I chatted with them, I soon realized they were all hungry. After a few questions, I learned they had not eaten anything all day. The government food program that normally feeds them lunch had closed for the summer because school was starting soon. Immediately, I remembered our emergency stash of food on the truck. I was so thankful I had restocked before coming. Even if I was absentminded and just going through the motions, I possessed the supplies for God to meet the needs of these kids. I started to make them sandwiches for lunch, and the kids were happily eating them as quickly as I could make them. I was so grateful we were able to meet this need. God had given us a plan earlier in the summer to always have our truck prepped and ready for hungry kids. Even though I wasn't intentional about meeting this need today, God was! Maybe that whole season of prepping the truck with extra food, even when we didn't need it, was for this very moment. God knew that by now it would be a habit for me, and these kids would need to be fed. I was so grateful the kids were able to see that they could count on God to meet their need. I was so grateful to be able to reach out in love to a bunch of hungry children and make sure their little bellies were filled. Physical hunger is sometimes just as painful as spiritual hunger.

While I was making the sandwiches, I looked down into the big brown eyes of a new child I had never seen before. I asked him his name as I slowly handed him a sandwich. He was a little nervous, but he was hungry. "Kevin. My name is Kevin," he quietly said. He took a few bites as I offered him a juice box. As he anxiously took it, I asked him where he came from and why I hadn't met him before. His response was one that will stick with me for the rest of my life. He told me he had spent the entire summer in a mental hospital.

In that moment, my heart broke for him. This small child, the same age as one of my own children, seemed to carry a heavy weight on his shoulders that no child should have to bear. I introduced myself to him and invited him to stay for the games we were getting ready to start. Since he hadn't been with us all summer, he had no idea what to expect, but he seemed to enjoy himself while he played enthusiastically with the other children and our volunteers.

After our game, it was time for the lesson. That day, I was teaching the kids a lesson that I am sure many of you have taught, about how we all have broken and bruised hearts because of what life throws at us. I showed the kids, with a giant poster board heart, what that looks like. I told them that each time someone says something that hurts us it leaves a mark on our heart. Each time something hard happens to us, a piece of our heart is ripped away. I asked the kids to give me some examples of things that had hurt them. By the end of the lesson, the poster board heart was barely recognizable. It was tattered and torn with marks all over it. The rips took away the very shape we had started with. I watched as my new friend, Kevin, wiped away a tear and became very quiet. I knew it was time to teach them about the brand new heart.

GO

Next, I showed the children a new poster board and told them about how Jesus not only wanted to heal their hearts, but to make their hearts brand new. As I prayed with the kids that day, Kevin responded to the love of Jesus. He surrendered his bruised and broken little life to Him and prayed to receive a brand new heart. The rest of the kids who were there had made similar decisions earlier in the summer, but this lesson helped them understand the process they were going through as they learned more about Jesus.

Kevin, very animated and excited, helped me pack up the truck afterward and had me write down on a piece of paper the day and time we would be back, so he could tell his grandmother. He wanted to be there early. You could see, almost immediately, the difference a full belly and a full heart made. As I drove away, I prayed over the fact that God had worked in and through our Sidewalk ministry, despite my lack of expectations.

As I was praying, God very clearly spoke to my heart. "I told you to go, but you didn't expect Me to show up." Ouch. That one hurt a little. You see, I didn't have a problem hearing God's voice when He called me to the streets to minister to the lost and hurting kids of our community. But I did have a problem when I refused to see that He was there, despite how I felt. He had planned that entire day, even down to the amount of supplies and food we had on the truck. I realized my obedience to go, even when I didn't feel like it, was what God used that day. My obedience. Some days we feel excited and charged and ready for anything, and then other days we feel like we are going through the motions and nothing big is happening. Yet, God showed me in that moment that He isn't looking for someone who is always happy, energetic, and fun. The reality is, sometimes we aren't. Even the craziest of kids' pastors have moments where they feel defeated, stressed, or overwhelmed. I think one of the biggest lessons I learned that day was that it's not about me. It's about Him, His plan, and

His purpose. On days when I have a great attitude, super fun games, and great prizes for the kids, the temptation might be to think that somehow I am responsible for the attendance or how receptive the kids are. But on a day like that Monday, God showed me how these are His kids, and no matter how I feel, He has a plan to reach the lost and hurting in our area. In a way, it takes some of the pressure off. When we realize our ministries are not dependent on us, but on Him, it helps us to take a deep breath and trust God with our kids. I believe God is not necessarily looking for the most talented people. I believe He is looking for the ones who will be obedient. Even on Mondays.

Beyond Our Expectations

I sighed heavily as I looked at our roster. We had more kids than last year—which was a good problem. Many of them, though, had been with us last Christmas when we were able to purchase shoes for them. We had been given a very generous donation from a ministry that provides shoes for kids who need them. Because we used the money wisely, we were even able to buy socks, candy, and a small toy to place inside the boxes with the shoes. This year, however, that would not be the case. Our supporter did not have the money to send us for our kids this year. As I looked through our list of names, I realized something very quickly. God knew every name on my list. He knew my heart for these kids. He knew their needs. So I did what I know to do—I prayed. I didn't pray some long, loud, elaborate prayer. Instead, I simply asked my Father for what I needed.

I had learned the previous season that part of my job is to expect God to show up and fill needs. This entire ministry has been 100% God's doing from the very beginning. In fact, the very reason we had shoes the year before was because God had provided them. So, instead of worrying about how I was going to pay for Christmas for our kids, I told God that I was expecting Him to show up.

GO

I started to go about my day, listening to voicemails I had missed overnight. The second message was from a woman named Carol, who was calling from New Jersey. Initially, I zoned out a little bit as I stirred some sugar into my coffee, but then my heart started to beat faster as I focused on what she was saying. She was calling from a ministry that focused on boxes of gifts for children, and the Lord had told her to call me. What in the world? Seriously? I called her back immediately, and as she started to speak, a tear ran down my cheek. I silently listened to her, thanking God as she explained her heart for ministry and the reason for her call. She and her husband, a retired pastor, had gathered toys for children and had gift wrapped them. She had seen our name in the back of a magazine and felt led to call and see if by chance we could use them. Of course, I told her that we could, and then briefly explained to her our Sidewalk ministry. She was so excited, and we ended our call with her promise to call me back once travel arrangements were made. They lived over 5 hours away, so she needed some time to make plans. As I hung up the phone, I thought about how some of our kids would have gifts now, and it took a little bit of pressure off of me. I wouldn't have as many kids to find gifts for. While I went about the rest of my week, I continued to pray about what to do for the rest of the kids.

The following Monday, I received a phone call from Carol. She and her husband would be there the following Thursday around 2:30 p.m. As I wrote the details down, I gave her directions and told her how thankful we were. Thursday came, and I counted up how many kids were on our Sidewalk roster. There were 130, plus a couple of additional infants who were not technically in our program, but were certainly under our influence. At least I would have a good idea of what I would still need to get after Carol dropped her gifts off. At 2:30, I went out to our front parking lot to peek out, and much to my surprise, I saw a large truck pulling into our lot. I ran out to meet them in the cold rain that was coming down. When Carol showed me what she had in the back of her truck, I was overcome with emotion. She had an entire truckload of wrapped and labeled gift boxes. They were even wrapped in plastic, so the rain would not ruin their wrapping paper. Carol apologized that she could not bring more and told me that they had brought about 130 boxes of gifts, plus about ten extra for infants in case we had any. 130! That was the EXACT number of kids on our roster! Very quickly, the Lord whispered into my heart, "More than you can ask or imagine." Ephesians 3:20 (NLT) then came to mind:

> *Now all glory to God, who is able, through his mighty power at work within us, to accomplish infinitely more than we might ask or think.*

I didn't even think to ask God about the babies on our list, but He knows their names. He sees them, and He loves them. "Yes, glory to You, God," I whispered back.

While Carol and I worked to put the boxes away into our storage shed, I was in awe of the time, care, and love she had placed into each box. She began to explain her process: "I start in March, and I pray over every single box. God knows what goes in each one, and I just listen. Then I pray about where God wants them to go."

I choked back tears as I explained to Carol about how we didn't have the shoe money this year like we did last year. I explained how at the very same time I was praying about our need, her voicemail was already blinking on my phone. It reminded me so clearly of what Jesus teaches us in Matthew 6:8 (NLT):

> *For your Father knows exactly what you need even before you ask him!*

Before I even had asked God about those Christmas gifts, He had already answered my prayer. Carol and I exchanged a hug, a few tears, and just a moment of worship as we realized what God was doing and

GO

how He had used each of us to reach His kids. In moments like that, all you can do is worship Him for who He is and how He loves.

Something to Think About:

I have learned several things as a result of these two events in our outreach ministry. The first is this:

As leaders in our ministries, we need to approach EVERY ministry opportunity with expectation.

If God has called us to do ministry, then there is a reason. He has an agenda. He has a plan. If we are offering ourselves as willing vessels, then we need to make sure we are expecting Him to show up. My challenge for you is to pray and ask God to reveal areas in your ministry where you have been going through the motions. Thank God for the fact that He wants to work in and through you to make an eternal impact on the life of a child. Then EXPECT that God will show up. I promise that you will see Him in ways you didn't before.

The second thing I learned through these instances is imperative to understand if you are going to last in a ministry like this:

This is God's ministry, not yours.

Yikes. I know that sounds a little harsh. I know we very often label our area of calling and training "my ministry." I want to ask you to take a few minutes right now to pray about that. I firmly believe there is power in our words. When we say it is "our ministry," we do something spiritually that can hinder the extent of our reach. We are placing a limit on how much ministry can actually happen. Instead, if we exchange our human limitations for a limitless God, how much more can we accomplish for the kingdom? This is "God's ministry." Surrendering in our hearts to the very one who calls us can have such a far-reaching impact on the communities we serve. God has more resources, more finances, more vision, and more love than we could ever hope to find on our own.

Obedience and Expectation. See how this combination impacts your ministry. You won't regret it. The only thing you will regret is not starting sooner. So just go.

11. REMARKABLE

Early in my ministry as a children's director, I would often feel burned out. I was working about 25 hours a week, and only a few of those hours were with kids. The rest were spent behind a desk, doing paperwork and various administrative tasks. I was teaching a pre-written curriculum I had inherited and was following the previous director's plan for record keeping, trying to prove myself worthy of my weekly paycheck. Each week, I would find myself exhausted, questioning if I were cut out for ministry, yet I knew I was called. Why was it so hard?

As I tried to keep up week by week, I realized I was going home from the church cranky and tired at the end of the day. Yet on Sunday evenings, after being with the kids for several services and oftentimes teaching an afternoon adult class, I felt invigorated. Those days were much longer, required much more of me, and had me going nonstop from start to finish. What was the difference? The difference was that on the days when I was teaching and ministering, I was operating in my gifting and calling. We each are called to fulfill a unique role in the body of Christ.

As I look at my schedule now, I am amazed at how different it is from a few years ago. I am a full-time director now, and most of my days are spent doing ministry on the streets of our community. I preach about 12 times a week and plan services for all kids, ages 0-12. Yet these days, I rarely experience burnout. As I meet children's

GO

directors and pastors from all over the country, the common theme I hear from most of them is that they are experiencing burnout. I came to understand one very important thing in those early years of ministry that I think is imperative to a long-term role in children's ministry:

We don't get burned out by doing too many things.
We get burned out doing the wrong things.

After a busy season of back-to-back VBS and camp, I had one day off after a nine-day stretch. Those nine days were filled with preaching, teaching, and one-on-one discipleship ministry to kids. When I had some down time, I read and studied God's Word and began to write curriculum for next fall's kickoff season. When I thought about previous years, I realized that in the past, a long stretch of work would have unleashed the cranky monster my family hated to be around. Yet this year I felt renewed and refreshed by writing a message that would inspire a new set of kids entering our fall classes. The major difference, regardless of the fact that I was working more and with greater intensity, was the fact that I was now operating in my gifting.

We are each uniquely equipped by God with a specific anointing that allows us to serve in a greater capacity in that role than in any other area.

> *Each of you should use whatever gift you have received to serve others, as faithful stewards of God's grace in its various forms.*
> 1 Peter 4:10 (NIV)

When we discover what our role is, we become aware that it is God's design for us to have joy while serving.

> *Serve the LORD with gladness! Come into his presence with singing!*
> Psalm 100:2 (ESV)

I realized early on that administration is not one of my gifts. Even the few hours a day I was giving to administration were enough to drain me of the joy of serving. I had a volunteer, however, who LOVED paperwork. Plugging her in to that role not only allowed me the opportunity to serve in a greater capacity with the gifts God has given me, but allowed her to be the part of the body of Christ that God created her to be. With the time I gained, I began writing and preaching my own kids' sermons. This gave me a greater sense of connectedness to the kids, and I was able to minister to their hearts with greater impact.

Sometimes we become so trapped into what we *think* our roles should be, we overlook or ignore the role God has uniquely designed for us. My challenge to you is to take a look at the things that are draining you. Once you identify them, pray for God to give you specific people to help take on some of those tasks. Delegate some of the things that you know you can let go of. My prayer is that as you do, you will experience the natural joy that comes with walking in obedience to the call God has placed on your life.

Focus First on God

One of the most important things we can do to stay focused on what God wants us to do is to maintain a close relationship with Him. I know that may seem obvious given the fact that you are reading this book; however, I have found while working in ministry that one of the hardest things to do is to carve out time for consistent and personal Bible study. I have to fight to get that time. People in children's ministry become so busy writing curriculum, planning classes, researching object lessons, and working on family devotions that we can very quickly sink into the assumption that preparing a Bible lesson counts as Bible study. It doesn't. Yes, you should be prepared for what you are teaching the kids, and you should have read and studied that portion of Scripture ahead of time, but that is for the kids. What will fuel you, your life, your ministry, and your passion is what God gives that is just for *you*. During those moments, while you are

GO

hearing from God, you will find the strength to stand when everyone else sits.

I learned this during our second year in outreach ministry. Every day, I drove past a certain mobile home park on my way to pick up my kids. I lived about ten miles out of town, and this neighborhood was pretty far from where we were doing our Sidewalk outreaches. When I drove by, I never saw any children, even though there was evidence that they lived there. The school bus stopped there, and bikes were in some of the yards. I began to sense that God was opening my heart to the possibility of starting an outreach there, even though it didn't seem to make sense. I had watched that happen once before at a location in town, but this place was basically in the middle of nowhere. As I prayed about it, the desire I had to reach this area grew stronger and stronger. I didn't speak about it to anyone—I just kept praying about it. One day, my husband came home from work and very bluntly said, "We need to start going to the trailer park up by the cornfield." He was talking about the same place I had been praying about. When I asked him to explain why, he told me about a young boy he had interacted with at work. Being in a public profession, he often sees children, but for some reason, he couldn't get this kid off his heart. He saw him later that same week at Walmart and learned that he lived in the trailer park we passed every day. This seemed to be a confirmation of what I had already been praying about.

So, praying for direction and wisdom, my husband and I continued to lift this neighborhood up in prayer and started talking about what an outreach there would look like. Over the winter, I got the proper permission from the park's owner, and the following spring, we presented the new site to the team. Saying we were met with resistance would be putting it kindly. This site was in the middle of nowhere. There were hardly any kids. It was a long drive. The time and resources could be better utilized in another area. Their excuses seemed to make sense; however, I was standing on what, by now, had become a very clear direction from God. I needed that direction in order to explain to our team why we were going there. To get them on board, I had to show them what God had shown me, both in prayer and in the Word. I am not confident I would have been able to do that had I not been studying the Word and listening intently to what God was saying. I'm not sure I even would have clearly heard the call if I wasn't paying attention. I believe God has put us in place, and we have a responsibility to maintain a posture of being upright before Him, intently listening for His direction. Without it, a lasting ministry that makes an impact for the kingdom simply cannot survive.

We set out to start ministering in that community the following month. The first week we had four children. This was the smallest group we had ever had, and we often had more adults than that on our teams. I could tell one of our volunteers was a little frustrated, even struggling with thinking that it was a waste. As I taught these little girls that God had given us that day, I taught as if we had a group of 100. I did not give them any less of me or of our program just because there were only four. The word from the Lord in my heart was clear: "These are the ones I sent you here for." I explained to our team that even if there were only one child, we would continue to come because God had a reason for calling us here. That site grew to be one of my favorites that year. Each week, we only had those four girls, but those four girls needed us. They were going through the bitter reality that they had been abandoned by their parents and were now living with their grandmother. Receiving time, love, and attention was exactly what they needed at a time when their world had been turned upside down. Every week, as we pulled in, the girls were there, waiting for us, jumping up and down in excitement. As we spent the summer ministering to them, we taught them how to pray, how to read their Bible, and how to worship. God had a plan for those little ones. Since that time, God has brought that family into our church family. They now attend regularly, and we are able to support them through all the hard things they face as they try to navigate emotions and struggles. I am so thankful I was able to hear God's voice when He called me there. He had a plan to reach those girls, despite the fact that it didn't seem to make sense to our physical eyes and plans.

God's plan is sometimes like that. We don't think it makes sense. That's why it is imperative that we keep a firm grasp on our relationship with Him, seeking Him every day for His plan in our life and our ministry.

The Good News Is for Everyone

One spring my oldest daughter was in a math competition along with other kids from her school. I didn't even know math competitions were a thing until I was signed up as a parent driver. My daughter goes to a Christian school, so most of the other parents who went along were also believers. As I sat at our table, waiting for the kids to finish up one of their rounds, I overheard a conversation between two mothers. I wasn't technically eavesdropping; they were sitting right next to me. I'm sure if I had wanted to I could have joined in the conversation at any time. But I didn't want to. One mom was complaining to the other about how her son had wanted to bring one of his friends, who lived in one of our low-income neighborhoods, to a church event. She went on to explain how she told her son he needed to "rethink" his decision. She appreciated that he wanted to reach out to one of "those" kids, but this was taking it absolutely too far. She simply *would not* drive her car down into that neighborhood. I couldn't believe what I was hearing. These were Christians. They were actively involved in a Bible-believing church. They liked and worked with children. They went on missions' trips. Yet here they sat, representing the reason so many of the kids in these neighborhoods are not reached. If these

GO

women could just get past *where* the kids lived, they would be able to see that they were just as loved and precious to God as the kids sitting in the room next to us.

That day was not the day to tell these women what I thought. Actually, we were supposed to be quiet since the kids were testing, and I knew if I started that conversation, it would be a loud one. Instead, I have committed to praying for God to break their hearts—for God to show them that His redemptive plan is not just for the people who line the seats of a pew or who live in certain areas. God's redemptive plan is for everyone. EVERYONE.

And then he told them, "Go into all the world and preach the Good News to everyone. Mark 16:15 (NLT)

Did you get that? The Bible says EVERYONE. Every single one. Are we taking that call seriously?

Something to Think About:

When my middle daughter, Adelyne, was very young, she realized the seriousness of the call to spread the gospel, as we explained it to her at our family devotion time. She was worried about our youngest daughter, who was just learning to speak. "What if Gracie died? Would she go to heaven?" she asked us worriedly. We explained to her about the concept of the age of accountability and that the baby was not quite old enough to understand the salvation message. We prayed with her and encouraged her to pray for her sister until the time came that she was ready to make a decision to follow Christ.

Later that day, I was doing laundry and went into the bedroom to put it away. I found Adelyne shaking Gracie, screaming at her, "Say you love Jesus! Say it!" Poor Gracie, not even knowing what was going on, mumbled in her best toddler language, "I love Jesus!"

Although this was a funny scene to come upon, it was clear to me that Adelyne "got it." Even though her passion was a little too

GO

intense, it showed on the outside what was going on inside. She was so concerned about the salvation of her sister she was willing to be persistent and do whatever it took to make sure her sister would come to faith in Christ. I wish more adults embraced this type of thinking when it comes to reaching kids in our communities. Too many times, we give up when an event doesn't get the results we want or our VBS isn't as well attended as we thought it would be. If those things don't work, we need to to try something else. Whatever you do, don't give up. If there is a need, there is a call. Find the need and go.

12. RESILIENCE

"I'm a Presbyterian!" the shout came. I looked at the screen door that opened into a dark room. I couldn't see anyone through it, but I could hear the anger in his voice. About once a month, I knocked on this door, just to ask if I could pray for the man who lived inside or to invite him to church. The very first time I knocked was the only time I had actually seen him. He had come to the door to see what I wanted but then told me very boldly that he grew up Presbyterian, so he didn't need to come to church. He walked with a limp, and there was sadness in his eyes. The neighborhood he lived in lent itself well to isolation, and he seemed content with living alone. An older man, probably in his early seventies, he showed his age. I knew he didn't have any children, so I didn't knock on his door during my weekly visits to the kids. I did, however, try to check on him at least once a month. Most of the time, he would see me coming, yell, "I'm a Presbyterian!" and slam the door. Sometimes I would catch him outside and just tell him I had been praying for him. He didn't quite know how to respond, but I never seemed to get anywhere with him. For whatever reason, God continued to lay him on my heart.

After this song and dance had gone on for at least a year, we were finishing up our mobile food pantry delivery at the end of the summer. We had almost an entire truckload of food leftover after we had delivered it to all the kids. Not wanting it to go to waste, I started at the beginning of the neighborhood and went door to door, asking

GO

the residents if they would like some of the leftover vegetables we had. Almost everyone did, and it blessed us to know the food blessed them.

As we drove into the Presbyterian's lot, I wondered if he would even come to the door. I walked up his steps and knocked, hoping he would at least let me speak. Out came the familiar voice.

"I'm a Presbyterian!" he shouted.

This time I yelled back, "Do Presbyterians like cabbage?"

"Cabbage?" he yelled back.

"Cabbage!" I shouted.

Suddenly, Mr. Presbyterian was standing at his door, looking out at me. I sheepishly held out a giant cabbage.

"I love cabbage," he said. He cracked open the door.

"Would you like two?" I asked.

"What else ya got?" he asked as he stepped out onto his porch. He maneuvered down his steps to our truck and about climbed into it. He grabbed a bag of potatoes, a bag of onions, and four cabbages. He started talking to our driver, and before I knew it, Mr. Presbyterian was laughing and joking around. I could hardly believe it. After all this time, after all these failed attempts, here was a man who was acting as if we were the best of friends. He began telling me how proud he was of us, reaching the kids of the neighborhood. He told me how he appreciated how consistent we were. He shared that he had, more than once, listened when we didn't know he was listening. Yet the door to his life had remained shut. Obviously, he was harboring some hurt, but today…today there were cabbages.

As I helped him carry his loot up to his house, I was amazed at what such a seemingly small gesture had done. I had prayed specifically for him for more than a year, and he didn't budge, but show up with the makings of a hearty soup, and I was his best friend. After he shut the door, I wandered back to the truck—still in a little bit of shock. "Cabbages for Jesus," I told my kids. We laughed all the way home that night.

I learned so much from that experience. It wasn't about the cabbages or the potatoes. It was about showing up even when things didn't go the way I wanted. It was about listening to the voice of God as He gently nudged me toward a man's door, knowing I was going to get a rejection. It was more about teaching me obedience and perseverance than it was about a slammed door. It was about meeting needs in whatever way possible in order to reach the lost. It was about reaching out after the one—the lost one—even if he didn't realize he had wandered off.

> *If a man has a hundred sheep and one of them gets lost, what will he do? Won't he leave the ninety-nine others in the wilderness and go to search for the one that is lost until he finds it?* Luke 15:4 (NLT)

As I studied this passage of Scripture, I realized that even though we were in that neighborhood to reach the kids, God had a plan to reach every single person who lived there. I still don't know Mr. Presbyterian's name. He hasn't told me. But now, he will smile sometimes and chat a bit when he sees me. Little by little, we are getting there. I don't know the extent of his hurt, but I do know the One who does, and I am thankful He has a plan.

A Ministry That Lasts

When I have shared my heart for this type of ministry at different churches or conferences, I always get questions about how to get an outreach ministry started. But truthfully, that's not the hard part. The hard part is how to sustain it. The majority of the work and ministry are not actually done on the platform during our program. Most of the "God moments" happen during the few minutes we spend with the kids outside of those times—the moments when we stop by the neighborhood just to check on them. That's when you find out kids

GO

are eating dog food for dinner, and you can swap it out for a pack of hot dogs. That's when you find a three-year-old outside with no adult in sight, and you stay until someone arrives to care for him. That's when you see the bruises that might have healed by next week. That's when you hear the arguments coming from the window and can offer a distraction so little ears don't hear.

By being consistent, no matter what it takes, you are able to offer something to these kids that is so much more valuable than any prize. You can offer them the chance to form a relationship with a trusted adult who genuinely cares for them. For some of these kids, this can be the difference that makes an eternal impact on their lives.

Last year, we witnessed God's hand on one of our families and realized our dedication to reaching this community had worked in favor of the kids. One mom in our neighborhood was struggling with a myriad of problems. There was some abuse in the home, addiction, mental illness, and genuine chaos. There were six children, most of whom attended our Sidewalk program. Through the relationships of our Sidewalk team, we were able to help support the family by taking the kids. The mom asked for our help because she didn't want the kids to end up in the system. As a result, four families, who are able to maintain a close relationship with each other, have the children. There is an open door for the kids to return to their mom, if or when she gets to the place where she is healthy enough to parent them. Until then, the kids are being loved and nurtured by caring adults with whom they already had relationships. The transition for the children into the homes of people they already knew and loved was so much better for them than if they had to go into the foster system. I believe this is truly the design for God's church. We should be able to stand up and care for God's kids in such a way that there is no need for the foster system. Yet bridging that gap for most churches has been so hard. Our role in getting the kids into safe homes is only possible because of the team being readily available and willing. Seeing God bring healing to a child who has not been able to stay with their biological parent has been one of the greatest rewards of this type of ministry.

As you embark on the plan that God has for your church, you will start to see the thread God is weaving throughout. That plan may look different for you than it does for me, but God has a plan for each and every person with whom you will come into contact. Who knows where it will lead, but really that isn't for us to worry about. Our part is just showing up and being available when God needs us.

Ministry Is All About Him

There she sat among the kids, staring at me reluctantly. Immediately, my heart beat a little faster. I was torn between wanting to throw my arms around her and wanting to yell at her for disappearing on me. Samantha. How many prayers had I sent up for her and her kids? Almost two years had passed since I had last seen her. Her kids had gotten bigger and her eyes more hollow.

I first met Samantha during our first year of Sidewalk. I actually met her children before I met her. As I looked down one day, two little arms covered in mud were raised up to me. This little one, maybe two years old, wanted held. As I picked her up, we started to dance to the song that was playing, and a smile came across her face. She was too little to understand the message we were teaching with our words, but she was certainly able to understand the message I was teaching with my actions. She just wanted attention and affection, so every week she and I would dance, smile, laugh, and hug. One day, after about three or four weeks, she arrived for Sidewalk with her little brother. He was equally adorable, and although he wasn't as interested in dancing, he loved being held. So every week I would look for my littlest friends, and I would spend time just giving them what they needed.

GO

One day, as we were dancing, I looked up and saw a young woman looking at me, watching me with the kids. Seeing the family resemblance, I walked up and introduced myself, asking if she was their mom. As what I suspected was confirmed, I found myself drawn to this mom and made it a point to remember her name—Samantha. From then on, I would seek out Samantha to check on her and to connect. I soon noticed that instead of standing in the back just to watch her kids, she had started sitting on the tarps with us and listening to the lesson. Every week I would offer a salvation message and prayer, and every week she would sit quietly without response. Samantha never missed a week, and she would always make sure her children participated, but for some reason, she remained closed off. She was kind, she was a good mom, and she paid attention and allowed the kids to have a great relationship with us. But time and time again, she would close up during the prayer. I would often take food from our church pantry to her home. She lived with her sister and their combined seven children. Samantha was often in and out of the hospital due to an ongoing health problem, but she didn't have to worry because her sister was always there to take care of her kids. I grew very fond of this family and would often drop by just to chat. I appreciated Samantha's friendship.

Some time later, I stopped by her neighborhood and knocked on her door. Much to my surprise, none of my little friends answered. Kids in the lot next door told me the family had moved out over the weekend. I was sad, but it was a bittersweet moment because when families move out I know that it is usually to go somewhere better. Still, I would miss Samantha and her children. God continued to lay Samantha on my heart, and I prayed for her often.

Two years later, we were starting Sidewalk at a new site. I was a little nervous because I did not know anyone in this neighborhood. I had been told there were children who lived there, but I had not made any personal connections yet. While I was blowing up balloons and getting ready to begin, I looked up to see a very familiar face staring at me. It was one of Samantha's children. I immediately looked around for her, and when our eyes met, we both teared up. Since it was already time to start, I went on with our lesson, and the neighborhood children responded so well. As soon as we were finished, I looked up to find Samantha standing by my side. I was honestly overcome with emotion. All of the time we had spent together in the past had not been enough to bring her to the point where she recognized her need for Christ. My prayer had always been that God would draw her near. After I lost contact with her, not knowing where her family had gone, my prayers had become more consistent. Now, as she stood in front of me, I could hardly believe it. She looked tired, and I recognized the heaviness in her shoulders. I told her how glad I was to see her and asked how she had been. Immediately, she broke down and told me about her sister, who had passed away the year before. Her rock, her best friend, was now gone. Through my tears, I asked Samantha if she was ready to come to the Lord. She nodded her head in agreement. She had been running from God for so long, and it was time for her to allow Him to give her peace and rest. I had the privilege of leading my friend to Christ that day. After I had long thought I would never see her again, God allowed me the honor of introducing her to the very One who could sustain her.

Sometimes we do not see instant results when we start pouring ourselves into the lives of others. It can take years of prayers and love before someone will open his or her heart. This can feel like a rejection, and quite honestly, sometimes we do get rejected. We go anyway. Sometimes people do not respond to us the way we want them to. We go anyway. Sometimes, no matter how hard we try, people slip through our fingers. We go anyway. That can feel like a heavy burden, and for a long time, I carried that burden. I wondered what I said that could

GO

have been said differently. I wondered if there was something more I could have done. My experience with Samantha taught me that it is not up to me to make people listen or believe. My only responsibility is to give them an opportunity to listen or believe. Coming to this realization helped me to understand that just as I am not responsible for the lack of faith in people, I am also not responsible for their steps of faith. Anyone who comes to faith in Christ does so because the Father has drawn him or her.

> *For no one can come to me unless the Father who sent me draws them to me, and at the last day I will raise them up.*
> John 6:44 (NLT)

It is not about me. It's not about you. It's all about Him. I believe that God used Samantha to teach me that all of our ministry work—every single moment—is about Him. That concept produces a humble spirit that I believe God is looking for as He appoints people as messengers of the gospel.

> *Humble yourselves before the Lord, and he will lift you up in honor.*
> James 4:10 (NLT)

When ministry is hard and doesn't seem to make sense, realize you are not alone in the fight—God is right there with you. The hard moments are the ones that are going to build resilience into you.

Something to Think About:

One cold and rainy December day, I needed to deliver shoes to every child in our Sidewalk program. I was at a site where the homes were pretty spread out. My daughter was with me, and after about ten minutes, we were both frozen to the core. As much as I loved the kids, I did not want to continue. The day was so bleak that I had a hard time even getting people to come and answer the door. When I stared at the boxes of wrapped shoes in the back of my van, I only felt defeat.

I knew these needed delivery, but I was already figuring out whom I could ask to bring them back down a different day. "One more," I thought. While we walked across the street to a child's home, a car drove down the road and sprayed us with muddy, frigid water. "That's it," I determined. We were going home.

Then, as I headed back to where I was parked, I looked up into the sky to see the most brilliant, spectacular, and bright rainbow I had ever seen. My daughter and I stood still, in awe of what God was displaying right in front of our eyes. In my spirit, I sensed God saying, "I'm here. You are doing My work. Keep going." As soon as it had come, the rainbow was gone. The day was so dark and cold that I am not sure anyone would have believed there had been a rainbow that day. But for me, that moment was just enough to encourage me and give me the dose of strength I so desperately needed. I hadn't thought to pray through the challenge since my body was so ready to call it quits.

When I look back on that day, I recognize it was one of many hard days. Sometimes there are simply days that well, "don't." Things don't happen as they should. People don't act as you expect. Props break, kids misbehave, neighbors interfere. But I sense those days are the very ones when we know that this thing is not about us—it's about Him. As God uses days like this to build resilience in us, we realize those challenges are simply distractions. Taking our attention off of them and focusing on Him allow us to fight whatever comes at us. In those tough spots, I look for the rainbow. Now, I know there is not literally a rainbow every time there are hard moments, but I also know that if I am stepping out in obedience to a calling God has placed on my life, then He is there. Sometimes I have to pause and look for Him, but He is always there.

When I share stories with people about what God is doing through this ministry, some people immediately are encouraged to jump into a similar ministry in their own communities and can't wait to get

GO

started. But sometimes people tell me that they think it will be too hard to do it in their area. I'm not going to lie; it will be hard. It IS hard. But that doesn't excuse us from doing it. Sometimes you have to start small, and your ministry may stay that way for a long time. You may not get immediate results. You may feel like you are taking three steps forward and two steps back. In fact, that's how it feels most of the time. This ministry is not glamorous, and usually, no one is standing there telling you that you are doing a great job. Many of the hours you put in are unseen, unacknowledged, and lead to heartache. And then…sometimes…you have a kid who tells you that if it weren't for you, he would be dead. Sometimes you have a kid who tells you that she shared the gospel with someone at school. Sometimes…you get a rainbow. But you won't find many rainbows inside the four walls of a church. Sometimes in order to see a rainbow, you have to get up and just go.

Appendix A

Sidewalk Sunday School

LESSONS

This section contains 12 sample lessons from our Sidewalk Sunday school program. Each lesson has a suggested game, music, lesson, prayer time, and prize time. Feel free to modify the lessons to meet your needs, or use them as a starting place for writing your own. At the end of the section is a sample attendance form. Make a copy for each week for each site you visit so you can keep accurate records for evaluating your program at the end of the season.

Sidewalk Sunday School • Lessons

WEEK 1: Mess

1. Games: Toilet Paper Gun (see Games Guide for details)

After rule review, select two boys and two girls to come up front. Using toilet paper guns, shoot toilet paper into the audience and tell kids to push it up front without ripping it. Kids up front are then to make one of the kids into a mummy. Whoever has the best/biggest mummy at the end (by vote) wins. Give each of the two kids on the winning team a candy bar. Make sure music is playing during game.

2. Music: (1) The Moving Song (2) We Came to Party

3. Lesson: Bad News vs. Good News

Tell a personal story about a time when you made a mess in your life.

We made a mess with that T.P., didn't we? What's the biggest mess you ever made?

Bad News First: Romans 3:23 (NIV) says that *all have sinned and fall short of the glory of God*. What do you think that means? What is sin? Have you ever sinned? Lied to your mom? Hit your brother or sister? Picked your nose? We all have, right?

Good News: Romans 6:23 (NIV) says, *For the wages* (What are wages?) *of sin is death, but the gift of God is eternal* (What is eternal?) *life in Christ Jesus our Lord* (Who was Jesus? Do you know what He did? He was God's perfect Son, and He died on the cross for you to pay for your sins! And then He came back to life! Now He is in heaven with God.) Say that verse again with me. Did you catch that? BUTT! We deserve death for our sin, BUTT...through Jesus we can live forever. Isn't that amazing?! All we have to do is believe in Jesus, that He died on the cross for us, and we can go to heaven with God too!

Sidewalk Sunday School • Lessons

4. Salvation and Response Prayer (A/B/C)

Close eyes/bow heads. We aren't looking around. This is between you and God. (A-Admit) I want you to think about the fact that you have messed up—we all have. (B-Believe) But if you believe that Jesus died on the cross for you, you can invite Him into your life so that you can live forever with Him. (C-Call) Say this with me: (Then lead kids in a prayer. After the initial salvation prayer, ask for kids to keep eyes closed. Ask if any have already asked Jesus to come into their lives but have since messed up and walked away from Him. If they have, then lead them in a recommitment prayer.)

5. Giveaway and Invitation to Next Week

As kids are leaving, have them line up in front of a leader. The leader will hand out the giveaway. The leader is to hand the treat to the child, not let the child pick it out. If kids want to trade after they get it for a different color, etc., that is fine.

Sidewalk Sunday School • Lessons

WEEK 2: Missing the Mark

1. Games: Frisbee Flyers (see Games Guide for details)

After rule review, choose 2 boys and 2 girls to make 2 teams. One child from each team will throw out 10 flyers. The other 2 children will be the designated catchers. The throwers throw the flyers into the audience. The audience then throws the flyers to the catchers up front. If the catchers catch the flyers, they then place them around their neck. The team with the most flyers at the end wins. Another version of this game can be played by blindfolding the throwers before allowing them to throw the flyers. Make sure music is playing during the game.

2. Music: (1) The Moving Song (2) We Came to Party

3. Lesson: We All Miss the Mark Sometimes

Did you like the game we played? Did the flyers land where they were supposed to every time? They missed the mark sometimes, didn't they? We've all missed the mark too. Some of us thought it would be really easy to get the flyer around your friend's neck...but yet we still missed.

We talked about sin last week. We are this week too. What is sin? To sin means to miss the mark sometimes. Sin puts us off track of where God wants us to be, just like missing the mark with the flyers put us in a different spot than where we wanted to be. Sooner or later, every one of us blows it. We mess up. The awesome thing is that we don't have to live in that place.... That yucky feeling you get when you mess up? God wants to clean up that feeling in us.

What are some examples of when you missed the mark? (Tell a personal story about when you did.) God has a bull's-eye that we always miss, but God NEVER knocks us off the team. We are His kids, and He ALWAYS wants us on His team. How is that possible? Colossians 1:13-14 (NKJV): *He has delivered us from the power of*

Sidewalk Sunday School • Lessons

darkness and conveyed us into the kingdom of the Son of His love, in whom we have redemption through His blood, the forgiveness of sins. ONLY GOD has the power to rescue us from being kicked off the team. How? He sent Jesus to be kicked off the team in our place. Once we invite Jesus into our lives, He rescues us from our failure.

4. Salvation and Response Prayer (A/B/C)

Close eyes/bow heads. We aren't looking around. This is between you and God. (A-Admit) I want you to think about the fact that you have messed up—we all have. (B-Believe) But if you believe that Jesus died on the cross for you, you can invite Him into your life so that you can live forever with Him. (C-Call) Say this with me: (Then lead kids in a prayer. After the initial salvation prayer, ask for kids to keep eyes closed. Ask if any have already asked Jesus to come into their lives but have since messed up and walked away from Him. If they have, then lead them in a recommitment prayer.)

5. Giveaway and Invitation to Next Week

As kids are leaving, have them line up in front of a leader. The leader will hand out the giveaway. The leader is to hand the treat to the child, not let the child pick it out. If kids want to trade after they get it for a different color, etc., that is fine.

Sidewalk Sunday School • Lessons

WEEK 3: We Were Made to Be Close to God

1. Games: Jumbo Stacks (see Games Guide for details)

After rule review, begin the relay race. Put cups on marked start line and mark an end line. Have kids run a relay where they go and grab a cup, run back, and stack it in a pyramid. Make sure music is playing during the game.

2. Music: (1) The Moving Song (2) We Came to Party

3. Lesson: Being Close to God

Did you guys like these buckets? Do you know what happened when we first got them? They were actually stuck together. Ms. Rachael tried to get them apart. Pastor Rich did. Pastor Joe did—actually he broke the yellow one trying to get it out. Ivonne did. Finally, as a team, we were all able to pull them apart. They fit together so well that they were all like one piece!

Those stuck buckets reminded me of something very important. Did you know that God created YOU to fit together with Him? Make a fist with one hand. This is like you. Put your other hand like this (hold hand out flat). This hand is like God. Now put them together and say WHOOP! (Slap flat hand around fist.) See that! You were created to fit together with God—just like that. Just like how those buckets fit together when we stack them.

But you know what? Sin...(What is sin again?) separates us from God. It's like this: Take your hands back apart and say Whoooo. Sin takes us away from God. How do we feel when we are away from God? What's the solution? Remember what I told you—that God sent Jesus for you? That Jesus wants to be your BFF? Well, Jesus is like superglue. Pretend to put some superglue on your hand. (Paint it on— swish, swish, swish.) Now, stick your hands back together like this: WHOOP! This is how they are supposed to be! When we ask Jesus into our hearts, when we ask Him to forgive us from all that yucky

Sidewalk Sunday School • Lessons

stuff that keeps us away from God, He becomes the superglue that connects us to God. John 3:16 (NIV) says, *For God so loved the world that he gave his one and only Son, that whoever believes in him shall not perish (die) but have eternal life.*

Do you have the Jesus superglue? What is superglue? Jesus acts like the superglue that keeps us connected to God forever.

4. Salvation and Response Prayer (A/B/C)

Close eyes/bow heads. We aren't looking around. This is between you and God. (A-Admit) I want you to think about the fact that you have messed up—we all have. (B-Believe) But if you believe that Jesus died on the cross for you, you can invite Him into your life so that you can live forever with Him. (C-Call) Say this with me: (Then lead kids in a prayer. After the initial salvation prayer, ask for kids to keep eyes closed. Ask if any have already asked Jesus to come into their lives but have since messed up and walked away from Him. If they have, then lead them in a recommitment prayer.)

5. Giveaway and Invitation to Next Week

As kids are leaving, have them line up in front of a leader. The leader will hand out the giveaway. The leader is to hand the treat to the child, not let the child pick it out. If kids want to trade after they get it for a different color, etc., that is fine.

Sidewalk Sunday School • Lessons

WEEK 4: Getting Knocked Down

1. Games: Giant Bowling (see Games Guide for details)

After rule review, divide kids into teams—boys vs. girls. One team rolls the ball while the other resets the pins. Each team rolls ten frames. Best score wins. This can be played more than once if desired. Make sure music is playing during the game.

2. Music: (1) The Moving Song (2) We Came to Party

3. Lesson: What Happens When We Get Knocked Down

Did you guys have a hard time knocking down the pins? They all pretty much got knocked down, didn't they? That reminds me of what happens to us a lot of times. We get knocked down too, don't we? We might get knocked down for real, like when someone pushes us, but sometimes we get knocked down when someone hurts our feelings. Has that ever happened to you? (Allow kids to give some responses, and then tell a personal story about when that happened to you.)

You know, when I was a kid, I had a hard time getting over it. Sometimes I still do. I feel like someone punched me in the stomach. I feel unloved. I feel like I wish those people who hurt me would just like me. Romans 9:25 (MSG) is one of my favorite verses. Do you know what it says? It says, *I'll call nobodies and make them somebodies; I'll call the unloved and make them beloved.* Do you know what beloved means? It means that God is WILD about you! That He cherishes you. You are His favorite! When I learned that, I realized it didn't really matter if those other people EVER liked me. Because who does? (God!) And God doesn't just like me! He LOVES me—a lot! He loves you too!

Sidewalk Sunday School • Lessons

4. Salvation and Response Prayer (A/B/C)

Close eyes/bow heads. We aren't looking around. This is between you and God. (A-Admit) I want you to think about the fact that you have messed up—we all have. (B-Believe) But if you believe that Jesus died on the cross for you, you can invite Him into your life so that you can live forever with Him. (C-Call) Say this with me: (Then lead kids in a prayer. After the initial salvation prayer, ask for kids to keep eyes closed. Ask if any have already asked Jesus to come into their lives but have since messed up and walked away from Him. If they have, then lead them in a recommitment prayer.)

5. Giveaway and Invitation to Next Week

As kids are leaving, have them line up in front of a leader. The leader will hand out the giveaway. The leader is to hand the treat to the child, not let the child pick it out. If kids want to trade after they get it for a different color, etc., that is fine.

Sidewalk Sunday School • Lessons

WEEK 5: Drenched in God's Love

1. Games: Water Relays (see Games Guide for details)

After rule review, divide kids into teams—boys vs. girls. Play one or more of these games: 1) Freezing Marbles, 2) Sponge Relay, 3) Slippery Soap, or 4) Frozen T-Shirts. Instructions are in the Games Guide. Or choose any other game where kids are sure to get wet. Make sure music is playing during the games.

2. Music: (1) We Came to Party (2) Whoa

3. Lesson: Drenched in God's Love

Are there any of us who are still dry? I need someone who is completely soaked. (Bring up a soaked child). Can any of you remind me what we talked about last week? We talked about God's love and how He calls us BELOVED. What does beloved mean again? This week we are talking about God's love again.

Have you ever had a time where you felt unloved? (Ask for kids to volunteer stories if they want to. Then tell a personal story about a time when you felt unloved.) You know, that feeling is terrible, isn't it? God showed me a verse in the Bible that made me feel a lot better. Can I share it with you? 1 John 3:1 (NIV) says, *See what great love the Father has lavished on us, that we should be called children of God!* And that is what we are!

Do you know what the word lavished means? It's an old word that means "drenched." Just like my friend—drenched to his underwear! That's a great picture of how much God loves you! SO much that you are drenched. Every spot is covered in God's love. Every. Single. Spot. The next time you don't feel loved, I want you to think of this moment—of what being drenched looks like—so you can remember how much you are loved.

Sidewalk Sunday School • Lessons

4. Salvation and Response Prayer (A/B/C)

Close eyes/bow heads. We aren't looking around. This is between you and God. (A-Admit) I want you to think about the fact that you have messed up—we all have. (B-Believe) But if you believe that Jesus died on the cross for you, you can invite Him into your life so that you can live forever with Him. (C-Call) Say this with me: (Then lead kids in a prayer. After the initial salvation prayer, ask for kids to keep eyes closed. Ask if any have already asked Jesus to come into their lives but have since messed up and walked away from Him. If they have, then lead them in a recommitment prayer.)

5. Giveaway and Invitation to Next Week

As kids are leaving, have them line up in front of a leader. The leader will hand out the giveaway. The leader is to hand the treat to the child, not let the child pick it out. If kids want to trade after they get it for a different color, etc., that is fine.

WEEK 6: Following God's Path

1. Games: Giant Kick Croquet (see Games Guide for details)

After rule review, divide kids into teams—boys vs. girls. Kids will kick balls through over-sized wickets. The first time play the game normally. Then play a second time with a child blindfolded, having to listen to the directions of the team to knock the ball down the course. Make sure music is playing during the game.

2. Music: (1) We Came to Party (2) Whoa

3. Lesson: Following God's Path for Your Life

Was it hard to get the ball to go where you wanted and to stay on the path? Was it easier or harder when you were blindfolded? Croquet can be hard because there is only one way, one path, that you have to follow in order to win.

Did you know that Jesus said there is only one way to receive eternal life, to live forever? It is only through Him. In John 14:6 (NIV) the Bible says: *Jesus answered, "I am the way and the truth and the life. No one comes to the Father except through me."* You know, when we were blindfolded, it was really easy to get off the path, wasn't it? In life we do that—we get off the path God has for us, and we kind of get lost. I remember a time I was lost. (Tell the kids about a time when you were lost.)

It's a scary feeling to be lost, isn't it? Even for just a few minutes. The truth is, without Jesus, we are lost forever. We become "found" when we decide to follow Him and He puts us back on the right path. Isn't it amazing that God loves us so much that He sent Jesus to guide us onto the path?

Sidewalk Sunday School • Lessons

4. Salvation and Response Prayer (A/B/C)

Close eyes/bow heads. We aren't looking around. This is between you and God. (A-Admit) I want you to think about the fact that you have messed up—we all have. (B-Believe) But if you believe that Jesus died on the cross for you, you can invite Him into your life so that you can live forever with Him. (C-Call) Say this with me: (Then lead kids in a prayer. After the initial salvation prayer, ask for kids to keep eyes closed. Ask if any have already asked Jesus to come into their lives but have since messed up and walked away from Him. If they have, then lead them in a recommitment prayer.)

5. Giveaway and Invitation to Next Week

As kids are leaving, have them line up in front of a leader. The leader will hand out the giveaway. The leader is to hand the treat to the child, not let the child pick it out. If kids want to trade after they get it for a different color, etc., that is fine.

WEEK 7: Friendship

1. **Games: Jumbo Matching Game (see Games Guide for details)**

After rule review, divide kids into teams—boys vs. girls. Kids take turns matching up pictures underneath cards. The most matches at the end wins. Make sure music is playing during the game.

2. **Music: (1) Whoa (2) How Great Is Our God**

3. **Lesson: Making Good Choices**

When we were doing the matching game, do you know what that reminded me of? I was reminded of how friends match up. We are going to continue with that.... Everyone find a partner. Now I want you to stand back to back. Now hook arms with your partner, and try to sit down. (Wait for them to sit.) Now stand back up. Don't forget to keep your arms linked! (Watch and encourage them.) Help each other; it's hard! (Wait for everyone to finish.)

Now I want you to stand face to face, about a foot apart. Try it again—only this time hold your partner's hands, try to sit down, and stand back up. Help each other. (Wait for them to finish.) Now everyone have a seat.

How did you help each other sit down and then stand back up? How is this like friends helping each other every day? (Let kids respond.) You were aware of your partner and how he or she was standing/sitting. You worked together to sit down and stand back up. You also had fun, right? Friends have fun together! There's more, though. Let's look at our Bible verse: Philippians 2:1-4 (MSG). *If you've gotten anything at all out of following Christ, if his love has made any difference in your life, if being in a community of the Spirit means anything to you, if you have a heart, if you care—then do me a favor: Agree with each other, love each other, be deep-spirited friends. Don't push your way to the front; don't sweet-talk your way to the top. Put yourself aside, and help others get ahead. Don't be*

Sidewalk Sunday School • Lessons

obsessed with getting your own advantage. Forget yourselves long enough to lend a helping hand.

The Bible tells us that friends help, encourage, and comfort each other. When friends need help, we help them. I'd like you all to stand up with your partner, and ask your partner in a moment how you can pray for them. Then we are going to take turns praying for each other. When we are done, we are going to pray together.

4. **Salvation and Response Prayer (A/B/C)**

Close eyes/bow heads. We aren't looking around. This is between you and God. (A-Admit) I want you to think about the fact that you have messed up—we all have. (B-Believe) But if you believe that Jesus died on the cross for you, you can invite Him into your life so that you can live forever with Him. (C-Call) Say this with me: (Then lead kids in a prayer. After the initial salvation prayer, ask for kids to keep eyes closed. Ask if any have already asked Jesus to come into their lives but have since messed up and walked away from Him. If they have, then lead them in a recommitment prayer.)

5. **Giveaway and Invitation to Next Week**

As kids are leaving, have them line up in front of a leader. The leader will hand out the giveaway. The leader is to hand the treat to the child, not let the child pick it out. If kids want to trade after they get it for a different color, etc., that is fine.

WEEK 8: Choices

1. Games: Giant Checkers (see Games Guide for details)

After rule review, divide kids into teams—boys vs. girls. Girls will be one color of checker; boys will be the other. Follow the typical rules for checkers. Make sure music is playing during the game.

2. Music: (1) Whoa (2) How Great Is Our God

3. Lesson: Making Good Choices

How do you win in checkers? What colors are the spaces? Black or white. Are there any gray spaces? Only black and white, right? You know, this week I was thinking about how that is a lot like life and the choices we make.

Did any of you make any choices today? When you got up this morning, what choices did you make? When you are at school or home, what choices do you make? We choose what we wear, when or what to eat, what to say, whether or not to listen to our parents or teachers, to be kind to our brothers or sisters, etc. So many choices.

How do you know if a choice is good or bad? (Let kids answer.) A bad choice would hurt others or yourself. Close your eyes for a minute and think about a bad choice you have made. Maybe you told a lie... or were mean...or stole something. Keep your eyes shut and listen. Psalm 119:105 (NIV) says, *Your word is a lamp for my feet, a light on my path.* Think about how hard it is to get around when we can't see, when it's dark. We need light in order to see where we are going, right? Open your eyes.

The Bible says that God's Word IS our light. There are always two options when we are making choices. We can try to stumble around in the dark, making bad choices because we can't see where we are going, or we can pray, ask God for help, read the Bible, and get some direction, like a light, for what we should do. When we need to make

Sidewalk Sunday School • Lessons

hard choices, the Bible gives us a clear, lighted path to make the right choice. I want to encourage you to listen to what we are teaching you at SSS and at church, and to pray before you make your choices so that God can help you.

4. Salvation and Response Prayer (A/B/C)

Close eyes/bow heads. We aren't looking around. This is between you and God. (A-Admit) I want you to think about the fact that you have messed up—we all have. (B-Believe) But if you believe that Jesus died on the cross for you, you can invite Him into your life so that you can live forever with Him. (C-Call) Say this with me: (Then lead kids in a prayer. After the initial salvation prayer, ask for kids to keep eyes closed. Ask if any have already asked Jesus to come into their lives but have since messed up and walked away from Him. If they have, then lead them in a recommitment prayer.)

5. Giveaway and Invitation to Next Week

As kids are leaving, have them line up in front of a leader. The leader will hand out the giveaway. The leader is to hand the treat to the child, not let the child pick it out. If kids want to trade after they get it for a different color, etc., that is fine.

… Sidewalk Sunday School • Lessons

WEEK 9: Connection

1. Games: Giant Connect Four (see Games Guide for details)

After rule review, divide kids into teams—boys vs. girls. Boys will play against boys; girls will play against girls. Play the game using the typical rules. Make sure music is playing during the game.

2. Music: (1) Jumpstart 3 (2) How Great Is Our God

3. Lesson: Made for Connection

When we were playing Connect Four, I had fun watching how you filled all those holes to win. As we were playing, it reminded me of something I learned when I was a teenager. (Tell a personal story about a time as a teen that you experienced a let down). I tried to make myself feel better. I tried music. I tried friends. I tried getting other people's approval. I tried Mountain Dew and Cheetos. I tried a bunch of stuff. And you know what? None of it worked.

I want you to take your hands and make a heart with them, right above your belly button. See that hole? I like to explain it like this. We all have this "God-shaped hole" in our lives. We can try to fill it with stuff. What are some things that we can try to fill it with? (Let kids answer.) Does any of that work? No! There's only one thing that can fill that hole! What is it? That's right! God's love! Even love from other people can't fill it! Do you know why? People can let you down. People can leave. People can hurt your feelings. Do you know who will never leave you? God! Do you know who will love you forever? You were made with that God-shaped hole, and nothing can fill that hole except God.

The Bible says in Romans 8:37-38 (NKJV), *Yet in all these things we are more than conquerors through Him who loved us. For I am persuaded that neither death nor life, nor angels nor principalities nor powers, nor things present nor things to come, nor height nor depth, nor any other created thing, shall be able to separate us from the love of God which is in Christ Jesus our*

Sidewalk Sunday School • Lessons

Lord. What is a conqueror? We can conquer loneliness with God. We can conquer feeling unloved with God. We can conquer being sad with God. Why? Because when we ask Jesus into our hearts and lives, He takes that hole and fills it right up with God's love. And NOTHING can separate us from that love. We were created to be connected to God.

4. Salvation and Response Prayer (A/B/C)

Close eyes/bow heads. We aren't looking around. This is between you and God. (A-Admit) I want you to think about the fact that you have messed up—we all have. (B-Believe) But if you believe that Jesus died on the cross for you, you can invite Him into your life so that you can live forever with Him. (C-Call) Say this with me: (Then lead kids in a prayer. After the initial salvation prayer, ask for kids to keep eyes closed. Ask if any have already asked Jesus to come into their lives but have since messed up and walked away from Him. If they have, then lead them in a recommitment prayer.)

5. Giveaway and Invitation to Next Week

As kids are leaving, have them line up in front of a leader. The leader will hand out the giveaway. The leader is to hand the treat to the child, not let the child pick it out. If kids want to trade after they get it for a different color, etc., that is fine.

WEEK 10 : Foundation

1. Games: Giant Jenga (see Games Guide for details)

After rule review, divide kids into teams—boys vs. girls. Girls will play against girls; boys will play against boys. Play the game using the typical rules. Make sure music is playing during the game.

2. Music: (1) Jumpstart 3 (2) How Great Is Our God

3. Lesson: What's Your Foundation?

When we were playing Jenga, did you notice how sometimes nothing happens when you take a block out, and other times the whole thing falls down? Why do you think that is? (Let kids answer.) The blocks that were not part of the foundation could be taken out pretty easily. But the blocks that WERE part of the foundation made the entire tower tumble when you took them out.

Sometimes things happen in life where we feel like we could just tumble, too, don't we? (Tell a personal story about a time where you felt like falling apart.) The Bible says in 1 Corinthians 3:11 (NIV), *For no one can lay any foundation other than the one already laid, which is Jesus Christ.* Jesus has to be our firm foundation. Without Jesus, we will crumble when life starts taking things from us. People say or do things that hurt us. Parents or teachers misunderstand us. We are hungry. We feel like no one cares. But guess what? Jesus is always there. He can help us through all of those things, and with His help we won't tumble. We will stand tall.

4. Salvation and Response Prayer (A/B/C)

Close eyes/bow heads. We aren't looking around. This is between you and God. (A-Admit) I want you to think about the fact that you have messed up—we all have. (B-Believe) But if you believe that Jesus died on the cross for you, you can invite Him into your life so that you can live forever with Him. (C-Call) Say this with me: (Then lead kids in

Sidewalk Sunday School • Lessons

a prayer. After the initial salvation prayer, ask for kids to keep eyes closed. Ask if any have already asked Jesus to come into their lives but have since messed up and walked away from Him. If they have, then lead them in a recommitment prayer.)

5. Giveaway and Invitation to Next Week

As kids are leaving, have them line up in front of a leader. The leader will hand out the giveaway. The leader is to hand the treat to the child, not let the child pick it out. If kids want to trade after they get it for a different color, etc., that is fine.

Sidewalk Sunday School • Lessons

WEEK 11: Temptation

1. Games: Tug of War (see Games Guide for details)

After rule review, divide kids into teams—boys vs. girls. Play a couple of rounds and, at least once, help one of the sides win. Girls will play against girls; boys will play against boys. Make sure to play music.

2. Music: (1) We Came to Party (2) How Great Is Our God

3. Lesson: Tug of War Once You Get to School

That was super fun, wasn't it? We wanted to finish up SSS with tug of war because we want to explain what happens once you go back to school. Tell me some things that you learned this summer at SSS. (Let kids have the opportunity to share). Once you go back to school, you are going to find that there are some people who might not like what you have to say about God, or they want you to start making bad choices again. Now that you have learned how to make right choices, to pray to God, and to listen for God's voice, it's important that you don't slip back into acting how you used to act before you knew about Jesus.

It's kind of like a tug of war. How did you feel when your team was pulled over the line? What happened when I (the teacher) helped one side? Have you ever experienced a strong pull or desire to do something wrong, even though you knew you shouldn't? That's called temptation. Did you know that, in the Bible, Paul described having that same feeling? In Romans 7:15 (NIV) Paul said, *I do not understand what I do. For what I want to do I do not do, but what I hate I do.* Then in verse 18-19 he said, *For I know that good itself does not dwell in me, that is, in my sinful nature. For I have the desire to do what is good, but I cannot carry it out. For I do not do the good I want to do, but the evil I do not want to do—this I keep on doing.* That's a guy in the Bible saying that! According to Paul, what is in us that makes us want to do wrong? What can we do about our sinful nature?

Sidewalk Sunday School • Lessons

Galatians 5:22-24 (NLV) says, *But the fruit that comes from having the Holy Spirit in our lives is: love, joy, peace, not giving up, being kind, being good, having faith, being gentle, and being the boss over our own desires. The Law is not against these things. Those of us who belong to Christ have nailed our sinful old selves on His cross. Our sinful desires are now dead.* Who can help us live the right way and make the right choices? How? (Let kids talk through this and then pray with them.)

4. Salvation and Response Prayer (A/B/C)

Close eyes/bow heads. We aren't looking around. This is between you and God. (A-Admit) I want you to think about the fact that you have messed up—we all have. (B-Believe) But if you believe that Jesus died on the cross for you, you can invite Him into your life so that you can live forever with Him. (C-Call) Say this with me: (Then lead kids in a prayer. After the initial salvation prayer, ask for kids to keep eyes closed. Ask if any have already asked Jesus to come into their lives but have since messed up and walked away from Him. If they have, then lead them in a recommitment prayer.)

5. Giveaway and Invitation to Next Week

As kids are leaving, have them line up in front of a leader. The leader will hand out the giveaway. The leader is to hand the treat to the child, not let the child pick it out. If kids want to trade after they get it for a different color, etc., that is fine.

BONUS WEEK: Falling Short

1. Games: Giant Kerplunk (see Games Guide for details)

Play this giant version of the popular game Kerplunk. Have boys and girls take turns pulling out sticks. This game can be played two ways: One version is the team who drops the first ball loses. The second is that the team that drops the last ball loses. Both are fun variations. Please watch the kids and have an adult collect the sticks after pulling them out so that the kids do not break the sticks or hurt each other with them.

2. Music: Select Kids' Favorite Songs

3. Lesson: What Happens When We Fail?

During this game, someone inevitably drops the balls to the ground and loses. No matter how careful we try to be when we pull out a stick, eventually the balls are going to fall and we fail. What are some other things that you have failed at? (Let kids answer. Then share a personal story about a time you failed, either as a child or an adult.) Our failures don't have to last forever. They are opportunities to learn and grow, as long as we are "failing forward." We take our failures as a step forward because they teach us a lesson.

The Bible says in Romans 3:23 (NLT), *For everyone has sinned; we all fall short of God's glorious standard.* It is normal to fail—we all do, and we need God's help. Without Jesus, we are separated from God, but with our belief in Jesus, we are able to live forever with Him. That also means He will help us on earth through His Holy Spirit. The role of the Holy Spirit is helper. He is here to help us whenever we need Him. All we need to do is ask.

Sidewalk Sunday School • Bonus Week

4. Salvation and Response Prayer (A/B/C)

Close eyes/bow heads. We aren't looking around. This is between you and God. (A-Admit) I want you to think about the fact that you have messed up—we all have. (B-Believe) But if you believe that Jesus died on the cross for you, you can invite Him into your life so that you can live forever with Him. (C-Call) Say this with me: (Then lead kids in a prayer. After the initial salvation prayer, ask for kids to keep eyes closed. Ask if any have already asked Jesus to come into their lives but have since messed up and walked away from Him. If they have, then lead them in a recommitment prayer.)

5. Giveaway and Invitation to Next Week

As kids are leaving, have them line up in front of a leader. The leader will hand out the giveaway. The leader is to hand the treat to the child, not let the child pick it out. If kids want to trade after they get it for a different color, etc., that is fine.

Sidewalk Sunday School • Evaluation

Date: _____ Kids in Attendance: _____

Site: _____ Adults in Attendance: _____

Leaders: _____ Salvations: _____

Did you visit kids this week: Y/N

How do you think today went overall?

What can you do better, or what goals do you have for next week?

How are you going to accomplish those goals? How can the program leader support you this week?

What moment made the most impact on you?

Appendix B

Sidewalk Sunday School GAMES

Many of the games suggested in this guide are available for purchase online. For a cheaper alternative, we partnered with a local Girl Scout troupe (Boy Scouts would be great too), and they made some of the games for us as part of one of their badges. They made our Connect Four, Kerplunk, Checkers, Matching, and Jenga. Not only was this a great way to partner with the community, it cut down drastically on our costs. Then, the Girl Scouts made additional sets and sold them throughout the summer to earn money for camp. It all worked really well.

You also could recruit game builders at church. These would make nice projects for your men's or women's ministry and youth group to help with.

WEEK 1: Mess

GAME: Toilet Paper Gun

- After rule review, select two boys and two girls to come up front.
- Using toilet paper guns, shoot toilet paper into the audience and tell kids to push it up front without ripping it.
- Kids up front are then to make one of the kids into a mummy. Whoever has the best/biggest mummy at the end (by vote) wins.
- Give each of the two kids on the winning team a candy bar.
- Make sure music is playing during game.
- Have kids help clean up toilet paper.

You can find many videos and instructions for making a toilet paper gun online.

Sidewalk Sunday School • Games

WEEK 2: Missing the Mark

GAME: Frisbee Flyers

- Choose 2 boys and 2 girls to make 2 teams. One child from each team will throw out 10 flyers. The other 2 children will be the designated catchers.

- The throwers throw the flyers into the audience.

- The audience is instructed to throw the flyers to the catchers up front. If the catchers catch the flyers, they then place them around their neck.

- The throwers then pick up the flyers the catchers missed and send them back into the audience.

- Keep going until all the flyers are used up or for a designated amount of time.

- The team with the most flyers around the neck at the end of the time wins. (This can also be played where the children actually have to catch the flyers on their neck.)

- Make sure music is playing.

Caution: Watch the flyers carefully because the kids like to steal them. There should be a total of 20 at the end of each game.

You can purchase flying hoops online—prices vary by the size you choose.

WEEK 3: We Were Made to Be Close to God

GAME: Jumbo Stacks

- Put cups on marked (chalk or tape, etc.) start line and mark an end line.

- Have kids run a relay where they go and grab a bucket, run back, and stack it to form a pyramid.

- Kids need to run back and tag the next member of their team, then that child stacks the next bucket.

- The goal is to be the team that finishes the pyramid first.

Make sure the buckets have a Lego block in them before putting them away. This helps them come apart more easily.

You can purchase a set of jumbo stacks online for around $30.

WEEK 4: Getting Knocked Down

GAME: Giant Bowling

- Create 2 teams—boys vs. girls.

- One team rolls the ball while the other resets the pins.

- Each team rolls ten frames. Best score wins.

- This can be played more than once if desired.

You can purchase a giant inflatable bowling set online for around $20-30.

Sidewalk Sunday School • Games

WEEK 5: Drenched in God's Love

GAME: Water Relays

FREEZING MARBLES: A kid's small plastic pool is filled with water, ice, and marbles. Four contestants have to stand in the freezing cold water and grab the marbles with their toes, then drop them in their team's container. Whoever collects the most marbles in their container in 2 minutes wins.

You can play this repeatedly, or do it relay style where kids each have to take a turn and then run back to the starting line.

SPONGE RELAY: Form 2 teams. Each team stands in a long line, facing the same direction. The first person dips the sponge into a big bucket of water directly in front of them. They pass this dripping wet sponge over their head to the person behind them and on down the line. The last person wrings the wet sponge into a container (which is directly behind them). Then they run up to the front of the line with the sponge and begin all over again. The team to fill their container first wins.

SLIPPERY SOAP: One member from each team starts this game. Hand each contestant a bar of soap. The goal of the game is to rub the soap in your hands and get it down to as small of a size as you can in an allotted time. The water is SOOOO cold (the same water used for the "Freezing Marbles" game) so have the players tag-team and pass the soap off to the next person in line when their hands get too cold or tired. (Set a time limit of 5 minutes.)

FROZEN T-SHIRTS: Ahead of time, freeze 2 wet T-shirts and some additional water in large plastic bags. When it is game time, hand one bag to each team and on "GO!" the teams have to break through the ice. The first team to melt the ice from the shirt and have one teammate put the shirt on is the winner.

WEEK 6 : Following God's Path

GAME: Giant Kick Croquet

- Create 2 teams—boys vs. girls

- Kids will kick large balls (beach balls or regular playground balls) through the over-sized wickets to complete the course.

- Follow typical croquet rules.

You can buy this game online for around $30-35. You could also make your own by using curved pool noodles or cutting hula hoops in half to make the wickets.

WEEK 7 : Friendship

GAME: Jumbo Matching Game

- Turn large cards face side down on the ground.

- Kids take turns flipping two cards over to look for a match.

- Alternate girls vs. boys.

- The team with the most matches at the end wins.

You can make this game yourself. You will need two identical pictures for each match and then adhere them to cardboard or poster board. You could also paint or stencil designs or patterns.

Sidewalk Sunday School • Games

WEEK 8: Choices

GAME: Giant Checkers

Basic checkers instructions:

- To begin the game, each player chooses a checker color and places their pieces in the dark-colored squares on their side of the board. The darker of the two colors moves first.

- Each player takes a turn to move one checker. In a normal move, a piece can move diagonally forward into an empty, dark-colored square.

- Pieces can also "jump" opposing pieces. To do this, an opposing piece must be in a square connecting to the checker you want to move, with an empty space beyond it. The moving piece jumps over the opposing piece and into the empty square. Remove the jumped checker from the board. If the moving piece can jump again, do so. A checker can move several times in the same turn.

- If a player has a piece in a position to jump, he or she must take the jump. If multiple pieces can jump, the player can choose which one to move. Forcing an opponent into a disadvantageous jump is a key part of checkers' strategy.

- A piece that reaches the starting row on the opponent's side of the board becomes a King. The player puts a second piece on top of it to indicate that it is a King. This piece can now move both backward and forward, taking regular moves and jumping in any direction.

- The game ends when one player has removed all of the opposing player's pieces. If one player has no possible moves remaining—for instance, if the only remaining piece is cornered by a double row of opposing pieces—the opposing player wins.

You can purchase a giant checkers set online for around $260.

Sidewalk Sunday School • Games

WEEK 9: Connection

GAME: Giant Connect Four

- Follow the instructions to set up the game.

- Players choose a color and place their discs on their side of the grid. Then take turns inserting a disc into the top of the grid. The first disc goes into the bottom row, but then players can place discs anywhere. The winner is the player who gets four discs in a vertical, horizontal or diagonal row. When the game is over, pull the bar at the bottom to empty the grid.

- Typically, you have the advantage if you take the first turn and put a disc in the middle column. This part of the grid gives you many options for play and limits your opponent's moves. You need a disc in this column to make any horizontal or diagonal line of four. If you don't have one, you can make only vertical lines. Corner squares are also good to have, but avoid edges, as they are too easy to block. Ideally, you want to build lines of three discs that have open spaces on either side, forcing your opponent to set you up for a win or leaving him with no way to block you in one move.

You can purchase a Giant Connect Four (Four Across) yard game set online for around $80 and up. Or if you have woodworking skill, you can build one using directions found online.

Sidewalk Sunday School • Games

WEEK 10 : Foundation

GAME: Giant Jenga

- Using the loading tray to hold them in place, stack the wooden blocks into a tower. Each level of the tower is made of three blocks laid side by side at right angles to the level below. Once you've placed all levels, carefully remove the loading tray. Whoever built the tower gets to take the first turn.

- Players take turns removing one block from the tower and placing it on top. Use one hand to remove blocks and do not remove them from the top row. Some blocks will be easier to move once play starts. Players are allowed to touch the tower to test which blocks will move. If a player doesn't choose to remove a block all the way, she must gently push it back into position. Once the tower begins to grow, players may only pull blocks from below the highest full row. If the tower still stands 10 seconds after the new block is placed, play passes to the next player to the left.

- Eventually, the tower will come crashing down. The player who last successfully added a new layer is the winner. The player who knocked the tower down sets it up again and will take the first turn of the next game.

You can purchase a Giant Jenga yard game online for around $80 on up. Or you can build your own using directions found online.

WEEK 11: Temptation

GAME: Tug of War

- You will need a long, fairly thick rope marked with a red line in the middle.

- Choose a grassy, level playing area and mark a line on the ground. Line up the mark on the rope with the mark on the ground.

- Divide up into equal teams. (If needed, play more than one round so everyone has a turn.)

- Line up the teams on each side of the rope. When the whistle blows, the teams will pull and tug, trying to keep their team on the correct side of the line.

- The game ends when one team is pulled over to the other team's side.

Caution: Don't do this game on cement/asphalt because someone always slips or falls down and then gets drug across the ground by the other players.

BONUS WEEK: Falling Short

GAME: Giant Kerplunk

- Set up the game tube. Insert sticks in a random crisscross pattern. Pour balls down the hole at the top. If any fall out the bottom, put them back in.

- Choose someone to go first. The player will pull out the first stick he or she touches. If any balls fall out, the player gathers them to count later.

- Continue removing sticks, one player at a time, until all of the balls have fallen out.

- Each player counts the balls in his or her pile. The person with the fewest is the winner.

You can purchase a Giant Kerplunk game online for around $30. Or you can make your own using directions found online.

Appendix C

Sidewalk Sunday School

LEADERSHIP TRAINING OUTLINES

The following sample outlines may be helpful as you train your volunteers. Feel free to adapt them to fit your audience or create your own. You will find that I have provided examples from my life to get you started, but you will want to replace those with your own experiences.

Sidewalk Sunday School • Training Outlines

What Does It Take to Work with SSS?

INTRODUCTION: What does it take to work with our Sidewalk Sunday school ministry? What leadership skills or other qualities are needed?

1. A genuine desire to work with kids

- Not necessarily talent—character is more important than talent
- Faithfulness/Loyalty/Good Attitude/Servant's Heart

2. Everyone has a part to play. We will find a job that fits your personality, but do not allow your personality to limit your job. God will stretch and grow you as you work with this ministry. Prepare for growth and be open to it.

3. Not everyone has to have the same time commitment, but we have the standard that you honor the commitment you personally have made.

- You can commit to a job: teacher, helper, prayer supporter, financial giver, meal maker, truck driver, etc.
- You can commit to a time: once a week, every other week, etc. Consistency is the key.
- You are not making a commitment to a leader or pastor, but are making a ministry commitment to God.

4. All positions are equally important

5. Visitation: Brief but consistent

- Contact (flyer)
- Faithful and short, not intrusive and long
- Expect to see God working and moving in these times
- This is when ministry happens—enables you to discern real needs (food, shoes, etc.). Sometimes people are just trying to take

advantage, but many times, people with real needs are hesitant to talk about them.

- Visitation is the key to establishing a long-lasting effect on your target community. It is critical in the process of getting families to church.

- Visitation is not house-to-house in the area you are working. Focus on the homes of kids who already come. (Blitzing is for every house in a neighborhood and will be done at different times.)

- Expect God to open doors to minister through these visits. Then step in.

- Consistent visitation builds bridges, which transport the gospel to where people are.

- Take the roster with you and update it as you go—sign up any new kids.

- Do not talk to people from your car—you don't want people to question your intentions.

- Do not take children anywhere in your car.

- Do not buy the children things. If you see a need or desire to sponsor candy/gifts/etc., it is best to come to the leader/pastor with your request.

- Do not wear sunglasses. People need to see your eyes.

- Be careful how you dress. We prefer you wear your SSS shirt. (Remember, you are their pastor.)

- Try to go at the same time every week.

- If no one is home, leave a flyer (not in the mailbox).

- Speak to the children and the families. (The goal is to reach the whole family.)

Sidewalk Sunday School • Training Outlines

PART TWO:

1. Prayer:
- Prayer is the foundation of every spiritual work.
- Pray like everything depends on it; then work like everything depends on it.
- SSS is a spiritual battle—expect predictable resistance.

2. Music:
- Pre-Service: draws kids in
- With games: ups the excitement, changes the atmosphere, gets kids engaged
- Worship: a tool to connect kids to Christ and evolves over the ministry season. Early on, worship time will be very simple. By the end, it will be child led.

Why SSS?

1. Evangelism: Take the gospel to places it hasn't been before and communicate it in a way that anyone passing by can understand.
- Relationship evangelism starts with relationship

2. Discipleship: As people get saved, they desire to get plugged in. They grow an appetite for God, Bible studies, bus ministry, church, etc.
- Reach a child, reach a family, reach a neighborhood, reach a community.

Sidewalk Sunday School • Training Outlines

How to Conduct a Sidewalk Sunday School Event

This lesson explains the general format of a typical SSS event. The elements we will be discussing should all be included, in this order. However, within this basic framework, feel free to expand and add your own ministry style.

Our SSS events follow the hourglass format ministry model: Fun/Serious/Fun.

Pre-Service: Upon arrival at the site, set up the truck and get things ready. First thing, set up the speakers and start playing some music. This will draw kids into the area. The louder and more fun the music is, the more kids will come. As some team members are doing this, other team members should be playing with the kids who gather. Things to have available for play: hula hoops, sidewalk chalk, bubbles, footballs, kick balls, etc. Engage kids—don't stand around talking to each other. This is the time and place to intentionally seek out kids to form relationships with them. This is a VERY important ministry opportunity that you do not want to miss. Have each kid fill out an attendance form and put them in a secure place. This serves as an attendance tracker as well as helps the children's ministry update the rosters.

Service Transition: About 5 minutes before the service begins, start saying on the microphone, "SSS is starting in 5 minutes. Grab your friends and come on down!!!" Repeat again at 2 minutes, then again at 30 seconds.

Welcome/Rules/Countdown/Prayer: Try to start on time. Eventually, you may have events scheduled at multiple sites on the same day, so it is important that you stick to the scheduled time frame. Start by welcoming the kids and asking them to have a seat on the tarp—boys on one side, girls on the other. Next, tell them your name and give them the rules. S-stay in your seat, O-obey your leaders, W-whistle means quiet. This will establish authority and allow you to get and maintain order over the group. Then do a blastoff countdown. After the whistle blows, everyone should be quiet, and you can pray or have a child pray to open the event. Have the person who is filling out the report (see sample on page 155) count the kids while they are seated. It's easier to keep track of them that way.

Worship Songs: After praying with the kids, work right into music and worship. "God Is a Good God" is a great song to start with; then maybe add a second song. Use whatever songs work well for you. In the beginning the music portion of the program will be hard because the kids may never have heard the songs, but they catch on quickly. By week 3 or 4, they should know the songs pretty well.

Object Lesson/Game: At this time, you will explain the game and play it. Games add even more to the event when they are object lessons that tie in to the theme for the day.

Game Connection: After the game is finished, bring kids back onto the tarps. Now that they have had a chance to play and exert some energy, it will be easier for them to settle down and be quiet. This teaching time does not have to be long. Typically, a child's attention span is about 30 seconds per year of age. So for 10 year olds, you would have 5 minutes to teach before they lose interest. Keep their attention by asking questions and expecting answers.

Response Prayer: Connect the lesson to the prayer. Always start with salvation—YES, EVERY. SINGLE. WEEK. When you feel like you are tired of repeating it, they will just be beginning to understand it. Then lead a second prayer in response to what you are teaching. Example: If we are teaching the Jenga lesson and talking about our foundation, ask the kids if they would like to commit to making Jesus the foundation of their lives. Do not get too caught up on the words—just help kids make the spiritual connection to the physical game or object lesson they just did.

Closing: After we pray, we always talk about how the angels have a

Sidewalk Sunday School • Training Outlines

party when even one child comes to faith in Christ. So do that! We give out a great big shout. You can do what works for you, but allow for a moment of "organized chaos" before dismissing (Fun/serious/fun). Also at this point, always remind kids that if they need prayer for anything they can raise their hands. Then send an adult to them. Before everyone leaves, do the attendance giveaway. Have an adult hand the item out to the children—do not let the children tell you what they want. They can trade afterwards if they want to.

Food: Food is last; otherwise, many kids will come for the food and then leave. Do not hand it out until last UNLESS you really know your kids and are confident they will stay. Feel free to hand out as much of the perishable food as you have—many kids will take extras for siblings or for other meals (sandwiches, not unlimited juice boxes).

SSS General Format:

1. Pre-Service Music/Bubbles/Chalk/Football/Hula Hoops/Forms
2. Service Transition Reminders starting 5 minutes out
3. Welcome/Rules/Countdown/Prayer
4. Worship Songs
5. Object Lesson/Game
6. Game Connection/Lesson
7. Response Prayer Salvation and then response prayers
8. Closing Handout and reminder for next week
9. Food

Sidewalk Sunday School • Training Outlines

Salvation and Young Children

Note: This is an outline of a message I shared with my team. I have provided examples in each section from my own life to give you an idea of what to say, but you will want to replace those with your own personal experiences.

Introduction: Highlight the topic, Salvation and Young Children, and a few key points that you will be discussing.

Scripture:

> *At about that same time Jesus left the house and sat on the beach. In no time at all a crowd gathered along the shoreline, forcing him to get into a boat. Using the boat as a pulpit, he addressed his congregation, telling stories.*
>
> *"What do you make of this? A farmer planted seed. As he scattered the seed, some of it fell on the road, and birds ate it. Some fell in the gravel; it sprouted quickly but didn't put down roots, so when the sun came up it withered just as quickly. Some fell in the weeds; as it came up, it was strangled by the weeds. Some fell on good earth, and produced a harvest beyond his wildest dreams.*
>
> *"Are you listening to this? Really listening?"*
> Matthew 13:1-9 (MSG), emphasis added

Types of Responses to Jesus

1. Scattered:

- *Study this story of the farmer planting seed. When anyone hears news of the kingdom and doesn't take it in, it just remains on the surface, and so the Evil One comes along and plucks it right out of that person's heart. This is the seed the farmer scatters on the road.* Matthew 13:18-19 (MSG)

- Maybe kids have heard the gospel from Grandma or on television. They simply couldn't "take it in" because it wasn't communicated to them in a way they could understand.

- Visiting church with my grandparents as a kid, I had no clue. All I knew was my knees hurt, it was long and boring, they said words I couldn't understand, and I was told to be quiet and sit still. The salvation message fell by the road.

2. Stony:

- *The seed cast in the gravel—this is the person who hears and instantly responds with enthusiasm. But there is no soil of character, and so when the emotions wear off and some difficulty arrives, there is nothing to show for it.* Matthew 13:20-21 (MSG)

- Some kids have been to VBS or visit a church once or twice but have no roots to dig down deep.

- I went to camp as a kid, responded to the message, but had nothing to help me when I came home. Back into the abuse, those spiritual things quickly faded.

3. Strangled:

- *The seed cast in the weeds is the person who hears the kingdom news, but weeds of worry and illusions about getting more and wanting everything under the sun strangle what was heard, and nothing comes of it.* Matthew 13:22 (MSG)

- Weeds come in the form of hard family situations and mixed messages from the outside world. Kids leave and wonder if the gospel "really works." They are bombarded with ideas like "money will make me happy," etc.

- Back into an abusive home, poverty, or just less than ideal parenting (working parenting, absent parenting, avoidance parenting), the child worries that this Christian stuff might not REALLY work. They have already been let down so many other times, so they reach out to what the world says works: money, jobs, selling

Sidewalk Sunday School • Training Outlines

drugs, popularity, expensive clothes, etc.

4. Salvation:

- *The seed cast on good earth is the person who hears and takes in the News, and then produces a harvest beyond his wildest dreams.* Matthew 13:23 (MSG)

- When a child hears and takes in the gospel, it produces a harvest beyond out wildest dreams.

- At the age of 15, I heard and felt the call to full time ministry. God is taking me places that this abused, neglected, and abandoned kid could never have imagined.

Sidewalk Sunday School Is Good Soil

1. What goes into good soil?

- Food: literal and spiritual. Kids hunger to be told they are loved and precious.

- Water: literal (juice boxes) and spiritual. God's Word provides cleansing/refreshing/quenching.

- SONshine: When we point kids toward Christ, they see clearly for the first time.

- Consistency: We are there every week, telling them the same thing.

2. We have to communicate the gospel in a way the kids understand.

- It's not just about hearing, but understanding.

- Head knowledge vs. heart knowledge

- I knew it before I came to church, but now I *know* it.

Sidewalk Sunday School • Training Outlines

Why Did Jesus Teach in Parables?

Why Tell Stories?

Scripture:

> The disciples came up and asked, "Why do you tell stories?"
>
> He replied, "You've been given insight into God's kingdom. You know how it works. Not everybody has this gift, this insight; it hasn't been given to them. Whenever someone has a **ready heart** for this, the insights and understandings flow freely. But if there is no readiness, any trace of receptivity soon disappears. That's why I tell stories: **to create readiness, to nudge the people toward receptive insight**. In their present state they can stare till doomsday and not see it, listen till they're blue in the face and not get it. I don't want Isaiah's forecast repeated all over again:
>
> Your ears are open but you don't hear a thing.
>> Your eyes are awake but you don't see a thing.
>
> The people are blockheads!
> They stick their fingers in their ears
>> so they won't have to listen;
>
> They screw their eyes shut
>> so they won't have to look,
>>
>> so they won't have to deal with me face-to-face
>>
>> and let me heal them.
>
> "But you have God-blessed eyes—eyes that see! And God-blessed ears—ears that hear! A lot of people, prophets and humble believers among them, would have given anything to see what you are seeing, to hear what you are hearing, but never had the chance. Matthew 13:10-17 (MSG), emphasis added

Sidewalk Sunday School • Training Outlines

Many of our kids had never had the chance to hear the gospel in a way they could understand. That's why we do what we do.

ABCs of salvation: Going to heaven is a SIMPLE as ABC.

A: Admit

- Admit you are a sinner.

- *All have sinned and come short of the glory of God.* Romans 3:23 (KJV)

Sinners need to acknowledge that they have sinned.

- Don't get too caught up on the words—use words kids understand.

- "I've messed up in my life."

B: Believe

- Believe that Jesus died for your sins, rose from the dead, and trust in Him alone for your salvation.

- *Believe in the Lord Jesus, and you will be saved.* Acts 16:31 (NIV)

All Jesus asks us to do to receive salvation is to believe in Him.

- "I believe, Jesus, that You want me to be Your best friend, that You loved me so much that You died for me and came back to life, so that You can help me in my life now and I can live forever with You in heaven."

C: Confess

- Confess your sins

- *If we confess our sins, he is faithful and just and will forgive us our sins.* 1 John 1:9 (NIV)

- We only need to tell Jesus that we have sinned and ask for forgiveness. Then He will forgive us, no matter what we have done.

- "There's yucky stuff in my life that keeps me from You. Please forgive me of that and help me to live for You."

Sidewalk Sunday School • Training Outlines

Salvation Statistics in Children

1. According to Barna Research[4], 76% of American adults consider themselves Christians.

42% of those consider themselves as born-again or saved.

An overwhelming percentage of those people experienced salvation before their 14th birthday.

2.

AGE	% who experience salvation in that age range
5-13	32%
14-18	4%
Over 19	6%

3. Should evangelism be concentrated on children?

Barna Research concluded:

- "The data also challenge the widely-held belief that the teenage years are prime years for evangelistic activity."

- Most church efforts to evangelize the unsaved is directed at adults—an age group which is relatively resistant to the message.

- They concluded that more evangelical programs should be directed at children and youth.

---

4 "Teens and adults have little chance of accepting Christ as their savior," Barna Research press release, 1999-NOV-15. This release is no longer available online. However, it was published in the 1999-OCT issue of Barna Reports, which can be ordered at: http://www.barna.org/cgi-bin/PageProduct.asp?ProductID=66

Sidewalk Sunday School • Training Outlines

Why Are Games Important in Children's Ministry?

Ice-breaker Discussion Questions:

Why do kids come to church?
Why don't kids come to church?
What keeps them from coming back to church?

Connection: Games are the tool we use to connect kids:

1. To each other:

- Interactive play connects kids to each other.

- They are disconnected because of the Internet, iPads, Xbox, etc. Sometimes they don't know how to connect with each other in daily life because there is such an emphasis on electronics in the homes. Even though we are dealing with kids who are in poverty, they still have access to electronic devices—sometimes more than to adequate clothing or shoes.

- We know that as believers we were made for connection.

2. To their leaders:

- Games open up kids' hearts. Once they expend physical energy, they are much more open to hearing what you have to say. Games are a tool to reach kids like coffee is to reach adults.

- Kids are starved for adult attention. Once you start establishing a relationship with them, you can start to minister to them. That's why we do consistent teams.

- Establishing authority: Rules without relationship breed rebellion.

3. To the message:

- Games give kids a visual, a point of reference, a connection to the biblical point.

- Make it relevant: Connecting Bible truth to their every day life.

- We try to connect the Bible concept for kids in three ways: learn by seeing, learn by doing, learn by hearing.

CPSIA information can be obtained
at www.ICGtesting.com
Printed in the USA
LVOW03s0006200717
541963LV00002B/2/P